T0332490

Praise for *Sink or Sit*
Jason and Haley Bilotti

When Jesus asked Jason and Haley to step out of the safety of the boat—to reach into the heart of Africa with His love and embrace His children—the Lord offered His hand to guide and protect them. *Sink or Sit* powerfully tells how their courage and commitment, with God's strength, transformed lives in Africa—and their own family.

—**Dr. John C. Maxwell,** #1 *New York Times* Bestselling
Author, Founder of Maxwell Leadership

I've known Jason and Haley for many years, and I've seen firsthand their passion for serving God and caring for others through mission work in Niger and elsewhere. With this book, many more people are sure to be inspired by the Bilottis' ongoing story of trusting God and stepping out in faith to share His abundant and abiding love.

—**Dan T. Cathy,** Chairman, Chick-fil-A, Inc.

Sink or Sit will leave you encouraged, inspired, and expectant for what Jesus can do with a life fully surrendered to Him. The Scripture tells us that we are to walk by faith and not by sight. Imagine what would shift in the world if God's people chose to put their Yes on the table. Jason and Haley have modeled trusting God with their Yes so well, and I pray their bold faith and trust in God will spread like a wildfire through this book.

—**Grant Partrick,** Pastor,
Passion City Church Cumberland

God determines the time and place a person will live ... so they seek and find Him. When they do, it's implicit that He invites them to help others seek and find Him too. He's bringing the nations to the light, and the Bilottis are making sure to walk worthy of God's call on their lives so that more and more people get to seek and find Him! Don't miss reading their story. It's been said, "If you want to walk on water, you've got to get out of the boat." Jason and Haley are doing just that, their gaze fixed on Jesus! Their story will inspire, challenge, and exhort you to leverage your life for the glory of God, to cover the earth the way the waters cover the seas!

—**Todd Peterson,** NFL Place Kicker, 1993–2006, and Chairman, Pro Athletes Outreach

This poignant and personal guide reminds us how God forms extraordinary faith through ordinary lives. These hard-won lessons will energize you on the path toward your own unique calling in the kingdom of God.

—**Katherine Wolf,** Author of *Hope Heals* and *Suffer Strong,* and Cofounder of Hope Heals Ministry

If you ever wondered how God might use an "ordinary" person like you, read this book! In *Sink or Sit,* Jason and Haley Bilotti nudge us out of our comfort zone as they share their compelling story, where time and time again, they refused to just sit, but instead, took the leap. As you turn each page, you'll become inspired to do the same, not someday, but today!

—**Tommy Newberry,** *New York Times* Bestselling Author of *The 4:8 Principle*

Haley and Jason Bilotti's story is truly remarkable and a great example of believers' faithfully answering the call of Jesus. *Sink or Sit* is an excellent reminder of how we must obediently respond to God's call and of the importance of bringing others who share that calling alongside us.

—**D. Michael Lindsay,** Ph.D., President, Taylor University

If you are lucky, one day you will have a chance to work shoulder to shoulder with Jason and Haley Bilotti. Reading *Sink or Sit* is the closest thing there is to that experience. You will laugh, nod, cry, underline, and share this book with your family and your team—I promise.

—**Chris Herschend,** Chair, Herschend Enterprises and Co-Founder and Managing Director of Elmwood Management

SINK OR SIT

One Couple's Journey of Answering God's Call to
STEP OUT OF THE BOAT

JASON AND HALEY BILOTTI

This book is dedicated to the ones who were willing to get out of the boat and walk on water for Jesus.

"Come," he said. Then Peter got down out of the boat, walked on the water and came toward Jesus.

MATTHEW 14:29

CONTENTS

FOREWORD

By Jeff Henderson

I've had my share of sink-or-sit moments, and I'm sure you have too.

Moments where your heart says, "Yes!" and your mind says. "Huh?" In fact, let me be honest. I talk to myself. (I have a feeling you do too.) And when it comes to moments of risk, moments that require a leap of faith, I find myself thinking and sometimes saying out loud, "I'm not actually thinking about doing this, am I?"

After all, sink-or-sit moments aren't for the faint of heart.

Sometimes, you have to leave.

Sometimes, you need to leap.

Sometimes, in the words of the great philosophers Van Halen, "You gotta go ahead and jump."[1]

What's interesting is that we often don't go looking for these moments. These moments often come looking for us. We're minding our own business and then suddenly, seemingly out of nowhere, we're faced with a sink-or-sit choice and opportunity. Should I take the leap? What if the water's cold? What if it doesn't work? What will other people think if I sink? Maybe I should just sit here, you know, "by the dock of the bay, watching the tides roll away..."[2]

I get it. The dock of the bay is a place of comfort. And yet what we often forfeit when we watch the tides roll away is an opportunity to make an impact.

In fact, here's what I've discovered about these moments:

Sometimes, the greatest risk isn't leaping.

Sometimes, the greatest risk is sitting.

Sometimes, the greatest risk isn't leaving.

Sometimes, the greatest risk is staying.

If your goal in life is to avoid risk, good luck. There's risk in everything. It's why Haley's opening question is so powerful: "Okay, Lord, what's Your plan here?"

If I can decipher God's plan and my role in His plan, that's always the best place to be. Oh, it's not the easiest, or even the safest at times. It's why I still try to abide by an adage a mentor of mine gave me years ago: "Don't ask God to bless your path. Figure out what God is doing and go there. That path is already blessed."

Sink or Sit is a story of two friends of mine who have done exactly that, and they found a path that has been powerfully blessed. I've known Haley and Jason Bilotti for more than twenty-five years now. This isn't theory to them. They have lived it. They don't sit on the dock of the bay. They have taken the leap. It hasn't always worked out perfectly. (By the way, it never does.) It hasn't always been easy. (Who said it would be?) But as you're about to see, it is always, *always* worth it.

But the goal of *Sink or Sit* isn't to share their story. The goal of *Sink or Sit* is to help you with your story. You see, sometimes, when we're overcome with fear and doubt about a sink-or-sit opportunity, it's helpful to borrow someone else's courage. Who said you had to rely on your own courage? When you run out of courage, it's helpful to borrow someone else's, even if it's just to take one small step forward. I can assure you. When you begin to understand the challenges Haley and Jason had to overcome in Niger, the courage inside of you will well up.

It's why this book is such a gift. It's a behind-the-scenes look at an amazing story of how the Bilottis joined in on what the Lord is doing in West Africa, but no one said sink-or-sit moments would be easy. Spoiler Alert: On their first trip back to Niger after COVID, well, let's just say things didn't go exactly as planned. When you decide not to sit but to jump, there will be moments where you to start to sink, where you feel like you're in over your head. It's all part of sink-or-sit moments—you're doing something you've never done before; the water is rising high.

It's why I often remind my kids of this quote attributed to T. S. Eliot: "If you aren't in over your head, how do you know how tall you are?"

You're taller than you think.

You're stronger than you know.

You're braver than you believe.

And while that's true, you'll never know this from simply sitting on the dock of the bay.

As I mentioned, I've known Haley and Jason for more than twenty-five years. I met them when I worked in marketing at Chick-fil-A. Six years into my career there, a sink-or-sit opportunity appeared. I was at a leadership conference in Chicago, and I felt like God called me to help start a church one day. As a preacher's kid, I had promised myself I would never, ever, never work at a church. But this calling was undeniable—much like the Bilottis' calling to help Niger.

And so, I had a choice—sink or sit?

The other day, I drove by the church Wendy and I eventually helped start. In fact, we ended up launching two other churches over the course of seventeen years before being called to another new sink-or-sit season. In those early start-up days, Haley and Jason attended our church. They were so encouraging to me. They supported us. I borrowed their courage on those days when I felt like I didn't know what I was doing. (Trust me, there were *lots* of days like that.)

I have battle scars from when things didn't go as planned. I have battle wounds of trying to keep up with how God was blessing our church. (Trying to keep up with the blessings of God is wonderful but also challenging!) But do you know what I *don't* have? I don't have regret that I didn't just sit. I jumped in. The waters rose. I was in over my head. But thanks to the Lord, and friends like the Bilottis, I found my footing and discovered I was taller than I thought.

I think that's what awaits you in the pages ahead. The goal isn't to convince you to make an unwise decision. The goal is to share this amazing story in order to give you courage when you need it, peace in the face of uncertainty, and perhaps, a gentle nudge. The tide is rolling away. And with it might just be the adventure of a lifetime.

So, what's it going to be?

Will you sink or will you sit?

If you need some help answering that question, turn the page.

PROLOGUE

J ason and I are ordinary people who try every day to walk in obedience to the Lord who opens doors and blesses us in ways we could never have imagined. On so many days, He takes me to places where I feel clueless—like when He led me to villages in West Africa, where I didn't speak the language. There, in a land that is 94 percent Muslim, He called me to speak the gospel. I prayed, "Okay, Lord, what's Your plan here?" Then He opened doors to a prison, an orphanage, schools, huts, and to the hearts of gentle souls who have become some of my dearest friends—and our son.

Jason was called by God to Niger, in western Africa, but for years, he and I traveled separately, as we had young children at home. Jason led groups of American missionaries in

January, and I led groups in October as we traveled to the same region every year.

The Lord put it on our hearts to write a book about His blessings. You will see that we are writing separately and together. That is the way God has allowed us to experience this adventure.

Our shared prayer is that you will hear and obey God's call for you and then step through the doors to adventure and blessing that He will open for you.

—*Haley*

The title of this book is *Sink or Sit*, but we originally considered the title *S.O.S.*, which might have stood for *Straight ahead or Sideways for Jesus*.

To us, *Straight or Sideways* means that one should always be striving to move straight ahead toward the arms of our Savior, Jesus Christ. We must know our true north and run toward it. "Straight ahead for Jesus" means having blinders like horses wear and staying focused on what God has called you to do. Wikipedia defines blinders as a piece of horse tack that prevents the horse from seeing to the rear and in some cases to the side. Many racehorse trainers believe these keep the horse focused on what is in front of him, encouraging him to pay attention to the race rather than distractions, such as other horses, crowds, fences, and so on.

Enough about horses—why should we wear blinders for Jesus? To eliminate distractions, right? They are all around us, and they come in the form of people, social media, television, other religions, obsessions, and idols. We know some of you are saying that you cannot see what's coming next with blinders on. In fact, visionary leaders say you must have peripheral vision to always be ready for what is coming next. While we agree with this, we are talking about having blinders for Jesus. Staying focused on what He has called you to do and running straight ahead into His arms.

Where does SOS originate from? On October 3, 1906, the SOS signal was established as an international distress signal by an agreement made between the British Marconi Society and the German Telefunk organization at the Berlin Radio Conference. The signal was formally introduced on July 1, 1908. In Morse code, SOS is signified by three dots, three dashes, then three dots (...---...). SOS was chosen because it could not be misinterpreted as being a message for anything else. It was sometime later that it was suggested that it might stand for "Save Our Souls."

So why did we name our book *Sink or Sit*? We want you to answer the call, say yes to Jesus, and trust that sinking is better than sitting. In his book *In a Pit with a Lion on a Snowy Day*, Mark Batterson writes about Peter and his choice to answer Jesus's call to leave the boat. Matthew 14:28 says,

"And Peter answered him, 'Lord, if it is you, command me to come to you on the water'" (ESV). Batterson writes,

> Peter is the disciple who sinks in the Sea of Galilee, but he was also the only disciple who walked on water. It's so easy to criticize Peter from the comfortable confines of the boat. I think there are two kinds of people in the world: creators and criticizers. There are people who get out of the boat and walk on water. And there are people who sit in the boat and criticize water walkers.[3]

Batterson also says, "I'd rather get wet than have a numb gluteus maximus. When everything is said and done, I think our greatest regrets will be the God-ordained risks we didn't take. We won't regret sinking. We will regret sitting."[4]

As we walk you through our journey in the chapters to follow, we hope you will see we were willing to leave the boat and possibly sink to answer God's call. Well, don't just sit there! Read on, and hopefully our story will challenge you to answer whatever God is calling you to do.

—*Jason*

ONE

CALLED BACK TO NIGER

HALEY: Jason and I drove to the airport with nine storage tubs packed tight for our trip to Niamey, the capital city of Niger in western Africa. COVID-19 was raging worldwide in January 2021, but according to the statistics, not so much in Niger. Our friends there wanted to see us, and I didn't want to wait another week to see them.

It's impossible to express in words the love God has given me for our friends in that desperately poor country in West Africa. I first met them on a short-term mission trip in 2008, and I returned for a week or more every year until 2020. Jason and I had each led more than a dozen mission trips there; he took a men's group every January, and I led a women's group every October. We adopted a child, fourteen-year-old Rachid, from an orphanage there. Rachid came into our Georgia home and became a brother to our children, Hunter and Paulina. I've visited women in prison; held sick and crying babies; danced, laughed, and played very competitive Duck, Duck, Goose games with the wives of local pastors; and I've washed the feet of women who walk miles every day in the red-orange dust that coats the entire landscape. God has even allowed me the opportunity to witness the birth of several babies in a clinic that is, at best, "acceptable" for a fourth-world country.

Jason and I worked through Effective Ministries, which facilitates approximately ten mission groups every year through its LINK Missions to serve people in Niger. My heart broke when COVID required cancellation of trips in 2020 and early 2021. Jason and I each had planned to lead a dozen American friends to minister in schools, churches, prisons, day cares, health clinics, and three different orphanages. I cried in October when the trip I was scheduled to lead was canceled, and I shared the idea with Jason that we should plan a trip on our own.

He thought we should wait. There was no COVID vaccine yet, and international travel was extremely difficult. In November, I brought up the idea again and we decided to wait at least until after Christmas. Jason is a Chick-fil-A franchisee with two restaurants in Atlanta. The dining rooms were closed, but the drive-thrus stayed open and busy. Being away from the restaurants for ten days was one thing, but if he was exposed and required an additional two-week quarantine, that would be much more disruptive. And with the holidays coming up, we didn't want to have to quarantine through Christmas.

Then Jason learned that Schools for Niger, Africa, an organization he and other Chick-fil-A franchisees created to build Christian schools, had been granted a $250,000 foundational gift. A grant this large would transform the lives of hundreds of Nigerien children, and Jason wanted to share and celebrate the news in person. We decided to go in January, and we started looking at travel dates.

Between us, Jason and I had traveled to Niger thirty-five times, but only three times together, when we led two summer youth teams and when we traveled to complete our adoption of Rachid. This would be a unique trip for just the two of us to do ministry. The Lord was giving us a beautiful opportunity. Without teams to share the work, though, we needed a different strategy.

With a team of twelve, we take as many as thirty-six Rubbermaid storage tubs filled with books and school supplies, Sunday school material, and items they can't get in Niger. We pack light for ourselves—three to four changes of clothes and minimal personal items—so we can carry more supplies.

Years ago, we made friends with a skycap, Lenny, at the Atlanta airport, and we always call him a week before we travel. Lenny looks out for us. He is waiting with two or three dollies when we pull up to the international departure curb. He makes sure a ticket agent is ready for us and our complicated check-in goes smoothly. The planning and logistics of getting a large group with dozens of big storage tubs to Niger is a lot more complicated than our days in the country, as we sometimes overcomplicate things on our side of the Atlantic. Or maybe they oversimplify in Niger. Here's an example of how simple life is in Niger: the mission group we work with helped a young man there create a micro-business selling produce from a garden. The young man had land by the river, and they helped him prepare and plant the garden. A few months later they went back, and his garden wasn't much bigger than a dining room table. They were alarmed and asked, "What happened to the big garden?"

"That was way too much," he said. "I didn't need all of that."

"But you were supposed to sell it. That was the plan."

"What I have here gets me through today," the young man said.

After nearly three dozen trips between us, Jason and I still don't fully understand that perspective, but we've come to embrace it for many of our friends in Niger. They live for today, and they will worry about tomorrow, tomorrow. Jesus said,

> Therefore do not be anxious, saying, "What shall we eat?" or "What shall we drink?" or "What shall we wear?" For the Gentiles seek after all these things, and your heavenly Father knows that you need them all. But seek first the kingdom of God and his righteousness, and all these things will be added to you. Therefore do not be anxious about tomorrow, for tomorrow will be anxious for itself. Sufficient for the day is its own trouble. (Matt. 6:31–34 ESV)

Niger is more than 94 percent Muslim, but they live at least one of Jesus's teachings. A favorite saying among our friends there is, "Americans have watches. We have time." I think of those words often. Jesus never had a watch.

Jesus spent His time on earth building relationships with ordinary people. Today, Jesus longs for us to spend time with Him and others. So before we took teams over, we talked a lot about building relationships, and the way we did that in Niger was by stopping and talking to people and spending time with them. Our friends there stopped and had tea with their neighbors and sat and talked with them for two hours before they went to the garden to gather what their family needed for this day.

I embrace that attitude, but if my family lived every day literally the way our Nigerien friends live, we never could have visited Africa. Planning a trip for just the two of us took weeks. Without a team to help shop and pack tubs for shipping, I managed lists and stacks for days.

Finally, on Wednesday, January 13, we were off, flying first to Paris on an overnight flight. We had breakfast during our layover at Charles de Gaulle Airport, then flew to Diori Hamani International Airport in Niamey. Upon arrival, the worldwide pandemic was evident. We stepped off the plane and encountered a man whose covering looked like that of an astronaut. He immediately began spraying our rolling suitcases, as well as our legs and shoes, with some type of disinfectant. After numerous sanitizing stations for our hands and the showing of our negative PCR test, we were allowed to pass through security.

We were greeted in baggage claim by our friends, Edouard, Edem, Ashley, Noah, and the LINK drivers, Mousa and Mohammed. My heart was overflowing to see each one of them, and as I embraced them, tears streamed down my face. It had been too long.

When you love somebody, sometimes you don't realize how much they love you back. On this trip, we experienced their love for us in a new way.

Every year, eight to ten groups of Americans visited the orphanages and schools served by LINK Ministries. Then in

2020, there were only two. So, when Jason and I arrived at the mission and visited an orphanage, kids ran toward us from every direction, arms wide apart, laughing and screaming for joy. They wrapped their arms around our legs, and when we bent over, they climbed up so that we had to hold tight to keep them from tumbling off.

We had been surrounded by COVID fears in the United States for almost a year, so we were more aware than ever of the children's runny noses and dirty hands and feet. I'd like to say that didn't matter to us—that we completely trusted God to keep us healthy as we did His work. But the thought crossed my mind more than once: If I continue to let the children come, I could become sick. Instead of pushing them away, we went through bottles of hand sanitizer and wore masks everywhere, especially inside. The adults there assured us that their infection rate was very low, although their testing was much less robust than in the United States.

Later in the evening I visited with Michel Mano in the kitchen. Michel manages the guest house where our groups stay when we're in Niger. We talked about COVID, of course, and how bad the spread was in the United States.

"Yes," he said. "When they told us you were coming, even in the middle of all that, we couldn't believe that you and Jason were coming."

"We wanted you to know how much we love and care about you all," I said.

You can tell somebody you love them. The words matter, of course. But these friends of ours are so dear to our hearts in ways that we could never express in words alone. So here I stood in a kitchen on the other side of the world in western Africa, loving with all the love Christ gave me for these beautiful people. Through them He had changed my life in ways that neither they nor I could have imagined.

JASON: Our trip did not go exactly as we had planned or hoped. We've learned in our years serving in Niger that when we dig in deeper and help Christ make a greater impact, Satan is real, and he shows up. On the other hand, if we don't see Satan and don't feel him scratching at us, then we're probably not going hard enough. Ephesians 6:11–13 says,

> Put on the full armor of God, so that you can take your stand against the devil's schemes. For our struggle is not against flesh and blood, but against the rulers, against the authorities, against the powers of this dark world and against the spiritual forces of evil in the heavenly realms. Therefore put on the full armor of God, so that when the day of evil comes, you may be able to stand your ground, and after you have done everything, to stand.

As we prepared to make the trip to Niger—a trip I had made eighteen times before with total confidence—I didn't feel 100 percent certain that it was the right decision. Frankly, I was afraid we might get stuck over there in quarantine. At this time the quarantine would be fourteen days in the LOC (LINK Outreach Center), where we stay with teams with spotty Internet connection, different foods, no television, and little to no interaction with the people on staff. This didn't sound really appealing to me, and the idea of missing two additional weeks for work and responsibilities back home wasn't sitting well with me. What if Haley tested positive? Would I be isolated from her as well? If I tested positive, would I encourage her to return home by herself? We were nine months into this worldwide pandemic, and Haley was asking me to go with her to a developing country. I had very little confidence that Niger was reporting its COVID cases correctly or diagnosing accurately, much less giving patients proper care. We love our friends in Niger, and we pray their government and economic system can someday lift them from their ranking as one of the poorest countries in the world. We have bolstered our prayers over the years with our love and our commitment to help as many people as possible, especially the children. But how much were we willing to risk?

Once Haley and I were on the ground in Niger, I was ready to visit with some of our Schools for Niger, Africa partners and get an update on construction projects of classrooms and upcoming needs, doing what I could to serve others and make an impact for Christ.

Then at midday Friday, I was feeling not quite right, a little nauseated as we visited one of our partners, Madame and General Wright at the STAR school. I decided it would be best if I skipped lunch. A couple of hours later, I started having cramps and diarrhea and throwing up. The episodes were intermittent and I didn't think I was in big trouble, but as the day went on and we got closer to dinnertime, I was in bad shape. I was hot and then cold, and when I tried to lie down, I began to have reflux; it wasn't something that a tablet of Tums would fix.

This had never happened to me on a previous trip. Don't get me wrong, I had been sick before from a virus or dehydration in Niger, but this was very different.

Our longtime friend Dave, an American missionary, came by to pick up supplies that we had packed for him and his family. Haley brought him into our room to speak with me. I was going downhill fast, and he insisted on taking me to the health clinic.

I don't remember a lot of details from that point. Haley was at my side praying when she wasn't advocating for me at the clinic. I was sitting outside the clinic behind a line of people under a dusty awning, cramping and thinking this was the place where I was going to die. I had been right all along, I thought, and I should have insisted to Haley that we not come. I was smart enough not to say the words out loud. Or maybe too weak to say them. I prayed, *God, either take me to my heavenly home now, or have the doctors fix me immediately.*

Suddenly, the creaky door opened, and a nurse called my name and took me in ahead of others in line. I thought, *All right, God, I guess You aren't done with me yet.*

The clinic was primitive. Like something from the early twentieth century. I sat at a table, and a woman who I hoped was a nurse pricked my finger to get two vials of blood. I would have expected her to take that much blood from a vein in my arm. Instead, she held a vial under my finger and squeezed to make the blood drip faster into it.

On previous trips, Haley had volunteered at a clinic farther out from the city, and she had a better idea than I did of what to expect. Hospitals back home have bright lights, shiny tile floors, gleaming stainless steel. This room was all in sepia, and I was blending in.

They said I needed an IV, but again, instead of accessing the big vein inside my elbow, she sank the needle between my right thumb and forefinger. The pain was overwhelming. Within minutes both arms were going numb and my hands were shaking uncontrollably. I thought I might be having a heart attack, and then the nausea came again, either from the pain, the fear, or the illness. I threw up violently into a large trash bag and then relaxed. The IV continued dripping saline, and when the IV bag emptied, they hooked up another. The feeling returned to my arms and the nausea subsided, and after two hours I felt more normal.

Food poisoning. Really? After spending my entire career behind the counter serving customers safely, I had encountered a bad egg or undercooked chicken while on the airplane from Paris to Niamey. Yeah, I know what you are thinking, the chicken salesman got sick from a chicken? Even God can have a sense of humor. Haley and I had eaten the same thing at every meal over the previous day except for these items on the plane.

Haley and I walked out of the clinic, and I felt close to normal, though weak. And I thought how easy it would have been in my pain to have said to Haley, "I told you we shouldn't have come." How painful those words would have been for her. She would have forgiven me, but the memory would have lingered.

Satan showed up when we were making an impact for Christ, when we were sharing His love with our dearest friends. Then Haley prayed for me, our friends prayed for me, and even the Holy Spirit prayed for me as He promised, and what began as a disaster was the beginning of a uniquely love-filled week.

In the same way, the Spirit helps us in our weakness. We do not know what we ought to pray for, but the Spirit himself intercedes for us through wordless groans. And he who searches our hearts knows the mind of the Spirit, because the Spirit intercedes for God's people in accordance with the will of God. (Rom. 8:26–27)

TWO

CALLED TO A MISSION

HALEY: I always wanted to do missions work. When I was growing up, our rural church south of Atlanta had a week-long revival every year, and each year a different missionary would preach. Sitting with my parents and my sister, I leaned forward and sat on the edge of the pew, enthralled by the stories the missionaries told. Most of them worked in the United States, but others told us of adventures across the world. I was always amazed at their stories of work with different cultures and I was inspired by their obedience to share the gospel wherever God had called them. That's what I wanted to do—what I felt called to do, even then—to share

Christ with anyone who would listen in the farthest corners of the world. "Here I am, Lord. Send me!"

I also longed to be a mom. I couldn't imagine a higher earthly calling. When I graduated from high school, I started college with a plan to become a kindergarten teacher—to spend my days with children.

Years later, when Jason asked me to marry him, I had no idea that God was working to fulfill my desires in ways I never could have imagined. God would allow me to become a wife, a missionary, a mom, and a teacher. All of that would unfold in God's time. God's perfect time.

JASON: As I prepared to graduate from Berry College in 1993, I applied for a full-time job with Chick-fil-A. I had started working at the Southlake Mall restaurant when I was fifteen years old, and I knew I wanted to make my career with the company. The day before I graduated from Berry, they hired me full time in what they called the Business Interim program, or B.I. for short. I would be traveling to restaurants around the country to operate on a short-term basis, somewhat babysitting the restaurant until Chick-fil-A selected a new operator. Or I might work with an operator to prepare for the opening of a new restaurant, usually spending six to eight weeks at each grand opening.

A week after I was hired, I proposed to Haley. We had met working at the Southlake Mall Chick-fil-A. Her sister,

Dena, was my age and had started working there about the same time I did. Three years later, Haley came to work at Southlake Mall when she turned fifteen. I was eighteen years old by then, about to start college. It would be nearly four years before we had our first date. At that time, I had been dating another young lady for quite a while, and I wasn't sure she was the woman I wanted to marry. One day I asked my mom, "How do I know when she's the right one?"

"Well, if you're asking me," Mom said, "then she's not."

I thought that was not very helpful, but Mom had just met Haley, and she knew she was special. It wasn't long before the other young lady and I broke things off and I asked Haley out.

She and I quickly fell into deep conversations, and I realized my mother's intuition had been right. Haley was special. She said she wanted to be a kindergarten teacher, and that was nice. But it meant three more years of college for her, and I wasn't sure I would be working and living near Atlanta for the next three years. I couldn't ask her to quit school and go on the road with me, so I didn't know how that was going to work. Then she shared what she really hoped for: to be a full-time mom.

That's the kind of home I always hoped to create, since it was what my mom and dad had decided was best for me and my brother, Chad, who is two years younger than me. When you're a kid, there's nothing like getting off the school bus and Mom having a snack ready—Little Debbie Oatmeal Creme Pies were my favorite—and having her oversee everything until bedtime. Having grown up in a family like that, I wanted a career that would allow my wife to stay home with our children. Haley wanted to be that kind of mom too. In June 1993, she accepted my marriage proposal and we set our wedding date for the following March. (I should probably mention here that I proposed to her wearing the Chick-fil-A Doodles mascot outfit in the Chick-fil-A Southlake Mall dining room. Yes, I was dressed up like a chicken!)

On Monday morning after graduation, I went to work for the Chick-fil-A B.I. program, traveling to several cities that summer helping operators open new restaurants. When David Thornsberry, who had been my first boss at the Southlake Mall restaurant, was named operator for a store at North Point Mall north of Atlanta and another freestanding store nearby, I was assigned to work with him to prepare for the opening. David needed to be near the soon-to-open store, and his family was still in Jonesboro, so he and I shared an apartment for a couple of months. I wish I'd had even more time with him, because during those days and nights I gleaned from him every bit of knowledge and wisdom I could about operations and leadership. The mall restaurant opened in October 1993, and I supported David with the opening of his freestanding restaurant in December as well.

Then, the following January, Ray Collins, operator of the Chick-fil-A in Hamilton Place Mall in Chattanooga, died suddenly and unexpectedly. He had gone home from work on Thursday night and had a massive heart attack. The company asked me to go up there to run the restaurant until they selected a replacement.

Ray was the brother of Jimmy Collins, president of the chain, and his death had an impact far beyond his restaurant. When I arrived at the restaurant on Monday morning, nothing on Ray's desk had been disturbed, not even his cup of coffee from Thursday afternoon. His staff was, naturally, distraught. His son, Mitch, was the general manager of the restaurant and was two years older than me. He wondered why corporate would send me in to run things. I understood and tried to walk lightly.

"I'm just here to serve and support," I said.

I stayed for two months, until Mitch was selected as the new operator. Then on March 5, Haley and I were married, and after our honeymoon, we hit the road for Chick-fil-A, heading west to Oklahoma.

HALEY: When Jason and I were engaged, I had just finished my first year at Gordon College in Barnesville, Georgia, and I decided not to go back to school. He was on a trajectory to become a restaurant operator, and I would be supporting him fully in that endeavor. From June 1993 until shortly before we married, I worked full time in the Southlake Mall

Chick-fil-A as well as a summer job working in a day care. Then in March 1994, when we came home from our honeymoon, Chick-fil-A sent us to Tulsa, Oklahoma. The operator there had lost his franchise because the restaurant had been run so poorly, and Jason's job was to figure out what had gone wrong, turn it around, and prepare the staff for a new operator. My five years working in almost every capacity at the Southlake Chick-fil-A prepared me to work alongside Jason.

When we stepped into the Tulsa restaurant, we didn't start making changes right away. Instead, we observed and made notes. After about seven weeks there, Jason had decided to cut any cost he could to try and make the restaurant profitable. He moved the two day-crew members we had to night shift, and he and I ran the restaurant from morning opening until 2:00 p.m. every day by ourselves. Since he was paid by corporate, I was the only employee counting for wages during these shifts. I can remember being so proud of ourselves, until our business consultant, Mark Moraitakis, came to visit and reminded us that we wouldn't be there for long, and we needed to prepare the restaurant with a trained staff for the next operator.

JASON: We were wrapping up our work in Tulsa when Mark came to town for a day. We went out for a jog, and I asked what was going on in his world.

"Well, I have a restaurant in a mall in Cleveland, and the lease runs out at the end of the year. Leadership in Atlanta thinks we ought to close it."

"Why?" I asked.

"It's not making money," he said. "It should be. I believe it could be. It's a good mall. But they've had seven interim managers in three years. Sales are up right now, and it's almost profitable, but if it doesn't start making money, they're going to shut it down. They just need the right operator."

I thought about all my extended family not far from Cleveland. After all, my dad had grown up in Pittsburgh, just two hours away. I'm a Steelers fan and a Penguins fan, and I was thinking I'd love to be an operator in Cleveland. If Haley and I could turn the restaurant around, maybe they would let me have the franchise.

"Send me," I said.

"Well, let's go back to the hotel and look at the numbers first," he said.

They were within three percentage points of profitability, and sales were rising. I looked at labor and food costs, the top two expenses that I could change immediately.

"Send me," I said again.

"Let me check," Mark said. I knew he needed approval from Atlanta to send me.

The next morning he called and said, "Okay, we're sending you. You've got nine months, and if you prove me right, that we should sign a new lease, I'll toot your horn from the tabletop to the rooftops. We'll try to get that restaurant for you."

I told Haley to pack her bags, we were going to Cleveland, Ohio!

HALEY: The mall restaurant in Cleveland was really bad when we got there. They weren't even following Chick-fil-A recipes. I walked into the kitchen, where the kitchen manager was whipping up something I didn't recognize—and I had followed every Chick-fil-A recipe hundreds of times. After a few minutes, I asked what she was making.

"Chicken salad," she said.

"Really?" I said, because it didn't look like any Chick-fil-A chicken salad that I had seen. "Can you show me the whole process, from the beginning?"

She did, and I immediately understood the problem. She was not de-breading the chicken before she chopped it, and the whole thing was just a grimy mess. It wasn't her fault. In fact, we felt bad for the employees, because nobody had trained them properly. Of course, the correct chicken salad recipe was something I could show her right away, but our first goal was to build relationships that would allow us to teach, train, and influence people in a way that is kind and loving. Jason and I had learned that in the homes we grew up in and also while working alongside David Thornsberry in his Southlake Mall restaurant.

Remember I said it was "really bad"? Picture this: Employees weren't in uniform. They weren't speaking to customers properly, and the whole operation was extremely disorganized. The second night we were there, I carried a pot of chicken noodle soup back to the kitchen before putting it away in the walk-in refrigerator, then went back out front to clean up. We sent the staff home and told them we'd finish cleaning and lock up.

A few minutes later, I went back to the kitchen, and the soup was gone. Somebody had walked out the back door with the entire pot, soup and all!

JASON: I had never done this before, and I haven't done it since, but after two weeks in Cleveland we had a really tough meeting with the staff. They had so much to learn, and it was time to enforce policies, starting with the easiest one: the uniform. We needed everyone to wear their uniforms correctly, and we needed men to shave and leave their earrings at home. "If you miss three of those over time," I said, "we'll have to let you go." Three strikes and you're out.

Customers at a restaurant chain expect the food and the service to be consistent wherever they go across the country. Otherwise, you don't have a brand. I had been brought up to be a good steward with what had been entrusted to me, and this opportunity to run a mall restaurant for Chick-fil-A was no different. Consistency began with the clothes or uniform the staff members put on before coming to work.

The next afternoon my night manager came in with no socks, unshaven, and wearing his earrings. I said, "One, two, three. I'm sorry, but you're fired." He just stood there incredulous, like I must be kidding.

"I'm dead serious," I said. "I'll close up the restaurant tonight." I know to some this may seem harsh, but I was black and white, and I meant what I said. We had to set the standard high and hold people accountable to get where we wanted to go. I wanted to be a good steward of what Chick-fil-A was asking me to do with this restaurant to get it back to the high standards that this brand deserved.

Of the twenty-seven people we had on staff, we had to replace fifteen. We began hiring right away, and we found people who enjoyed working with us and who liked serving customers. Then they started recommending their friends for jobs. We were profitable our first month, and by October our sales were up 40 percent. The turnaround was so dramatic that Jimmy Collins flew up from Atlanta to see what was going on at this restaurant they had been planning to close.

Sales and profits kept rising, and in December Mark came up, took Haley and me out to dinner at an amazing neighborhood pizza joint, and told us, "If you still want to be two hours from Pittsburgh, the restaurant is yours. We've re-signed the lease, and from what I see, you're going to kill it. You're going to quadruple your income."

We were actually going to get our own restaurant?! This was exactly what we had been working for. Then Haley started crying. Not just crying—bawling as she tilted her head into her hands.

Mark and I sat quietly for a moment, and then he said, "I think I have my answer."

I responded quickly, "No, no! Wait! Let us think about this. Let us pray about it. Give us some time."

I knew, of course, that Atlanta was home for Haley, just as it was for me. We had talked about that when we considered the possibility of getting this restaurant. Then in the moment, with the offer on the table, it all became real to her. We wouldn't be going back home, and that reality was crushing to her.

I didn't like the idea of saying no to the offer. When would the next one come along? And where would it be?

I called David Thornsberry and asked for his advice.

"You don't want to be in Cleveland," he said flatly.

"What do you mean, I don't want to be in Cleveland?" I said.

"You want to be in Atlanta, right?"

"Sure, but I don't know if I can get an Atlanta restaurant. We can start here right now."

David said he was confident that we would have an opportunity in the Southeast if we were patient.

Haley and I prayed about it, and ultimately we felt God guiding us away from Cleveland. I told Mark no, and we hoped and prayed for another opportunity. One thing that helped us make our decision was that snow had been covering the ground for some seventy days straight during that long, cold winter.

Two months later, in February 1995, the company announced it was opening a new freestanding restaurant on Northside Parkway near West Paces Ferry Road in Atlanta. It was clear from the beginning that I didn't have a shot for that one. They would want a successful operator with more experience to take that location. But my name stayed in the mix, and Mark started tooting my horn, just like he promised.

Then some concerns arose about the location that may have discouraged some operators from pursuing it. The store would have the highest rent in the chain. And because of the upscale location, some were concerned that it might be difficult to recruit team members. Also, Chick-fil-A was still primarily a mall-based chain in early 1995, and a lot of operators were not sure freestanding restaurants would perform as well. I was thinking, *Let's take a risk; after all it's home, and I drove by that site for years heading to and from Berry College!* All of this, along with Mark's cheerleading for me, had an impact on the decision, and in June, they told me that I would be operating the new restaurant. I was twenty-four years old, and we were coming home.

Early on, as Haley and I worked together in the restaurant, we balanced each other's personalities. Haley was extremely high on compassion, and she was all about loving the employees. We hired a lot of teenagers to work in the restaurant, and Haley was like a younger mom to some of them. They could share their problems with her, even cry with her, and she'd probably cry with them in return.

After twenty-nine years of marriage, I'm still learning Haley's number one message: it's not always what you say, it's how you say it.

Haley was in the restaurant with me every day, and when I saw an employee was struggling, I would ask her to talk with them. With compassion, she would help them understand issues they needed to address. But working in the restaurant wasn't her long-term plan.

HALEY: When North Point Community Church was founded in 1996, Jason and I began attending. The congregation didn't have a building yet—Sunday services were held in a temporary location. We attended this church for many years and served in many different roles. Over time the church began sending groups all across the world on short-term mission trips—exactly what I wanted to do!

God had given me a heart for His children, and I longed to tell them about Jesus—to share the love of Christ. Jason and I were young, and though we planned to have children, we didn't yet. The time seemed right to me.

Jason was more cautious than I was, at least where my physical well-being was concerned. He said he didn't feel comfortable with me going to a developing country, especially with people or organizations we didn't know. I could have pushed back, and he might have relented, but that's not the kind of marriage we have. I was disappointed, but God had plans that I couldn't see.

JASON: Chick-fil-A restaurants are, by design, small family businesses. Truett Cathy, founder of the brand, always wanted it that way. In many cases, like ours, operators' spouses also work in the restaurants. For our first five years of marriage, Haley and I were both spending fifty or sixty hours a week in the restaurant. That sounds crazy, but we loved our staff and our customers, and we loved working together, so why not?

It wasn't until I went on a long-planned hunting trip to Alaska with my dad, though, that I learned the operation didn't require my attention every moment of every day. For twelve days I was out of contact in the brush on horseback. Our general manager, Lawson Bailey, and Haley were running the restaurant.

I thought about them every day, wondering how things were going, but I had no way of contacting them.

When I came home and stood in the restaurant, I thought, *It's still here.* They had sold just as much chicken with me gone for a while. I was humbled at first but then inspired by the idea that we had developed a strong leadership team. I began focusing on leadership development, reading books by John Maxwell and other leadership experts. "Everything rises and falls on leadership," Maxwell says.

Here's an example of my self-revelation: Whenever I was in the restaurant, I made sure all the stock was neat and straight. If I left and returned, I would often find that the stock wasn't straightened, and I would straighten it again. Well, that was my own fault, because I was the only one who ever did it. I had to teach and delegate what I was expecting if I didn't want to do it all myself or if I wanted it to continue smoothly while I was away.

Then Haley became pregnant with our first child. It was a joy and a milestone we'd been dreaming of, and she kept her schedule at the restaurant until a month or two before Hunter was born. Her first calling was to be a mom, but even after Hunter was born, she came into the restaurant a few hours a week to handle billing and some other responsibilities. We scheduled those tasks at times when I could go home and stay with Hunter.

It didn't take long for the stress of that juggling act to wear on us.

Haley and I were friends with many of the Atlanta-area operators, which gave us an opportunity to see and learn from decisions they made running their businesses. Two particular operators and their wives were about our age. Both couples had children, and one of the wives stayed home. The other got back involved in the business and was practically running the restaurant.

Haley could have followed either model and succeeded. She had strong relationships with our staff, she was a fantastic businesswoman, and she was strong with the finances. But we both knew her passion was to be a mom. We were talking at home one night, and I mentioned the two wives and their decisions. "They represent our choices," I said. "Which one do you want to be like? Because it looks like you're becoming the strong, full-time businesswoman, but that's not what I thought you wanted."

"I know," Haley said. "That's not my passion."

HALEY: When I left the store to come home full time, my life revolved around Hunter's schedule. I might take him out for a couple of hours and then make sure we were back home in time to keep him on his feeding schedule. He and I did everything together, and I loved every minute of it. Two and half years later, Paulina was born, and it was like God had given us the perfect family. We had a boy and a girl, two wonderful children. Our family was complete. My dream of being a full-time mom had come true, and my heart was full.

JASON: I was watching the movie *The Family Man* shortly after Hunter was born, and in one scene Nicolas Cage was looking into a crib at a baby. It just tore me up, the love I felt for our little child. I had heard for years that the love you feel for your own child is different from anything you will ever experience. It was true.

Then I realized that maybe I could better understand our heavenly Father's love for us. When I held Hunter, I knew I would do anything for him, even die for him. I don't know if I could have said that before he was born. Anytime our children are hurt, I feel their hurt. I can't stand to see them in pain.

HALEY: I could have become isolated with them in the house. I was a mom twenty-four hours a day, and I needed connections beyond that responsibility. Hunter was four years old and Paulina was two when I learned about Bible Study Fellowship, or BSF. I joined a group that met at a church in Cobb County. Many of the participants were moms, so there was childcare available at the church. BSF met weekly, and the women's group I joined had more than five hundred members who divided into smaller groups for study and fellowship. Then we came back together for teaching from Linda Olmstead, a brilliant woman whom God had gifted with talents for teaching and leading.

I immersed myself as completely as possible, reading and studying the lesson every week, and I looked forward to the Wednesday morning class.

As I was trying to figure out the calling the Lord had placed on my life, I was tempted to look around at the Christian women who surrounded me and think, *Wow, I don't have the gifts that they have. I could never do what they do.* I knew this was nothing but a trap from Satan, yet I was entangled so easily in comparison.

The Lord gently reminded me that He designed each of us uniquely the way He wanted us to be. He gave me the spiritual gifts He wanted me to use on my journey with Him, and He showed me that He does not make mistakes. Where He calls, He equips. Therefore, I need not worry, for He has the plan and all the tools I need to complete the course set before me.

Then in April 2006, after I had been a part of BSF for two years, Linda asked me to serve as a discussion leader. The responsibility would be significant—more preparation and an additional meeting on Tuesdays to pray and discuss the week's lesson with other group leaders. God made it clear to me through my prayers that He had created this opportunity for me, and He wanted me to accept it. So in the fall of 2006 (BSF takes summers off), I began leading a group of women through the book of Romans.

Only years later would I realize the many ways God used BSF for His purpose. He took me deeper into His Word every week to strengthen my understanding and my relationship with Jesus; He continued to develop my leadership skills week by week; He gave me new friendships with a strong group of Christian women; and then, years later, He used those friendships to encourage dozens of women to travel to Niger with me and share the love of Christ.

God also gave me prayer partners through Bible Study Fellowship. The power of their prayers strengthened me to lead. Cheryl Hash and I met when we were training to be first-time BSF leaders, and we soon discovered our daughters were the same age and both loved horses. Cheryl and I brought our daughters together to play, we took long walks, and we prayed together. Cheryl soon became one of my most important prayer warriors as I tried to understand God's call for Jason's and my life.

Hunter was reaching kindergarten age, and my desire for our children to have a Christian school experience similar to my own, with loving, prayerful teachers grew stronger. Jason and I toured Whitefield Academy, where the children in a kindergarten class were sitting in beanbag chairs with Christian music playing softly. The teacher had each child come to her to read. We watched for a while, and as we turned to leave the room, we overheard the teacher praying with one of the children. That moment touched my heart, and I could feel the presence of the Lord there and across the campus. Hunter started kindergarten there, and our family began a long, wonderful relationship with the school, the parents, and the students.

JASON: In 2001, a young man working with me at the restaurant decided he was going to build a library for a village in Africa. Little did I know that God was planting a seed within me for what was to come in the continent of Africa. The young man made a proposal: if I let him sell Chick-fil-A chicken biscuits in the morning at Whitefield Academy, he would take the profits and use them to build that library. I agreed, and for years we delivered biscuits every Tuesday and Thursday morning to Whitefield from our restaurant, about twenty minutes away.

In 2006, when Chick-fil-A made plans to open a restaurant in nearby Vinings, I asked to be considered as the operator. It was a long shot. From the inception of Chick-fil-A, founder Truett Cathy had limited operators to just one restaurant each, because he wanted us to be in our restaurant interacting with customers and staff. Later he allowed operators to have two or more restaurants in special circumstances. I hoped that the proximity to our existing restaurant, my commitment to developing leaders, and the fact that our kids were at Whitefield, just five miles away, might help sway the decision.

Every day I drove over to the empty lot where the new restaurant would be built, and I prayed for the opportunity, if it was God's will. I had always worked hard and prepared for an additional opportunity; I was never one to just sit idle. I was about action, and stopping to do this prayer every day on the way to work was another way for me to step toward this opportunity.

While the restaurant was under construction, I was invited to join seven other Chick-fil-A operators on a trip to Galveston, Texas. When a couple of guys stand around a grill, the conversation will usually drift to sports, family, business, and sometimes faith. Or fishing. We had gone deep-sea fishing earlier in the day, and we made more than one reference to Jesus's apostles fishing in the Sea of Galilee while we were out in the Gulf of Mexico. We caught plenty of fish, but Howe Rice and I were grilling steaks for ourselves and the others back in the house.

Howe was an operator with two restaurants in Richmond, and I was eager for the opportunity to ask him about managing two restaurants—what were the challenges? Instead, he told me about Niger, Africa. We could talk business later, he said. As I spent time with this group, I learned that one operator was supporting an orphanage in

Russia, one operator had just adopted two boys from Africa, and Howe was pouring into Niger. I felt convicted and challenged to do more, as I shared with the group that I was attending church and Haley and I were leading a small group in our homes on Tuesday nights. I needed to do more. I had to do more.

Niger had completely changed the trajectory of Howe's life. He visited the country for the first time in 2003 with a group from his church, and he was stunned by the poverty he witnessed. He knew going in that Niger sat with Haiti at the bottom of the world's nations economically, but to see how the desperately poor people there were actually living touched him deeply. He had compassion for them and felt the Lord telling him, "I want you to leverage your business to impact this nation."

To understand what that message might mean, Howe asked his hosts how he, a Christian, might help a country that was 94 percent Muslim. Church buildings could help, they said. So could health-care facilities. But schools could make the greatest impact. Particularly middle schools. Most Nigerien students ended their education after elementary school because they had to take a test to move on to middle school, and a huge percentage of students failed the test. The Christian elementary schools did a good job of preparing students for these exams, and Muslim families were willing to send their kids to those schools because they were superior to government-operated schools. But they needed more: more classrooms, desks, and teachers.

A new middle school in the country, he learned, would cost $100,000 to build and open. That was a huge challenge, and Howe didn't want to start if he didn't believe he could succeed. In fact, he couldn't succeed unless God gave him the success. Then he thought about the apostle Peter, when Jesus told him to get out of the boat and come to Him. Was Howe's faith big enough to attempt the thing God was asking him to do? Would he get out of the boat and trust God?

He prayed and he believed, then he reached out to his customers to help. He hosted Niger Night in the restaurant, and he hung a map of Niger on the wall. His staff caught his passion, and when they told some of their regular customers about the effort, checks started rolling in. Some big checks— $1,000 and more.

But even that wouldn't be enough to build a school. He asked his staff to brainstorm ways to raise more money for the school. Big ideas.

Howe's marketing director said, "How about a dodgeball tournament?"

Howe chuckled but then realized she was serious.

"No, really," she said. "Dodgeball."

Howe said he would pray about it—ask God for guidance—but he was skeptical. Not long after that, God gave him the answer. Howe was up in the middle of the night with his newborn son. He turned on the television, and ESPN was broadcasting the National Amateur Dodgeball Tournament. The sport, they said, was exploding. "Thank you, God!"

The next day Howe and his team began working on the first Chick-fil-A Dodgeball Tournament. They raised $68,000 to help build a school for children in the poorest country in the world. A year later they raised $88,000.

The steaks were almost done. The smoke was drifting away on the tropical breeze, and Howe had a question for me. Was I ready to get out of the boat? Would I go with him to West Africa in November and meet God's children in Niger? Would I be open to God's call in my life for those children?

THREE

CALLED TO SERVE GOD'S CHILDREN IN AFRICA

JASON: My new restaurant was scheduled to open in the fall, the same time frame Howe wanted me to go with him to Niger. I told him there was no way I could leave the country for a week in the middle of the opening, and he understood, having opened two restaurants himself. To be honest, I was a little relieved. I wasn't sure God was calling me to make that trip. I have learned that when we choose fear, we miss out on opportunities in life and God's plan for us. But if we choose bravery, we get to live in step with God and experience the fullness that life has to offer.

Just a few weeks after Howe invited me, my restaurant opening was delayed, but by then I'd missed the opportunity to travel with him. He had needed a commitment months in advance so they could get the best group rates on plane tickets and so the team could train and plan for the trip.

In late summer he called again. Somebody had dropped out of his group, and he knew about our delayed opening. "We have one spot left," he said. "You can come, but we need to know right away."

Suddenly it felt like God was removing the obstacles and clearing the way for me to go to Niger.

HALEY: When Jason came home from Texas and said another Chick-fil-A operator had asked him to go to Niger, I was confused. Jason had never indicated personal interest in international mission work. His conversations with Howe seemed to have changed him. He wasn't ready to buy a ticket to Niger, but his heart was stirring.

Then a few months later, when the restaurant opening was delayed and he decided to go, I turned to my friend Cheryl to share the conflict in my heart. Of course, I wanted Jason to go, but I was the one who had a lifelong desire for international mission work, and I knew that desire was my response to God's call on my life.

When I told Cheryl about Jason's trip, I began to cry. We were at BSF, and I couldn't explain my tears with so many people around. I was upset with God for sending Jason first and not me, and at Jason for responding to the invitation. I didn't want my disappointment to turn to bitterness, and I wondered if God would ever send me. All that confusion was wrapped up in feelings of guilt for making it all about me.

Cheryl and I went to lunch, and as we talked more about Jason's upcoming trip, I began to feel more confident that God would be calling me soon. Maybe I would go to China, where BSF founder Audrey Wetherell Johnson had served as a missionary in the 1930s. I didn't know. I only knew that I wanted to be obedient and to trust God. So I prayed, and I waited.

Cheryl reminded me of Abraham, who took his family and left his home to follow God's call, and of God's promise to Abraham, who was old and had no children. God told him, "Look up at the sky and count the stars—if indeed you can count them. . . . So shall your offspring be" (Gen. 15:5).

Abraham waited such a long time for the promise to be fulfilled! Yet he remained faithful—so faithful that centuries later, Paul reminded the Romans, "Abraham believed God, and it was credited to him as righteousness" (Rom. 4:3).

Cheryl told me, "Haley, don't look down at your dusty sandals. Look up at the stars and look at all of the promises God has for you."

And that's what I tried to do. Being a full-time mom to Hunter and Paulina was what I wanted and what God had called me to be. Yet God continued to touch my heart with His call to share His love through international missions.

"I'm sure He wants me to go somewhere," I told Cheryl when we were walking one morning. "I don't know where He's taking me, but I need for you to pray for me."

JASON: Effective Ministries began sending LINK Missions teams to Niger in 2003, and when I joined Howe's group in 2006, they had developed an efficient system of training and planning for weeklong trips so that we made the most of every day in the country. I participated in several hours of training with our group, learning about the country, the people, the weather, the expectations, and much more. But I wasn't *really* prepared.

When we landed at the Niamey airport, the ground crew rolled a stairway across the tarmac to the plane, and then a flight attendant opened the door. Heat poured into the cabin of the plane like an oven. I walked down the stairs, and I immediately knew this place was different. We made our way through customs, and our translators and drivers guided us through the airport to the parking lot, where we were surrounded by children tapping us, and saying, "*Cadeau? Cadeau?*" That is French for, "Gift?" They were begging, and it was breaking our hearts.

That night, November 3, 2006, I wrote in my journal:

As we walked out of the "airport," an old, tattered, concrete building that was clearly in a fourth-world setting, kids were begging with bowls all the way to our van. The van trip to the Bible school, where we would stay, was indescribable really. Poverty at its worst! Huts and thatch shacks, and people everywhere just walking with old shaggy clothes. The whole city was orange dirt with hardly any green, no grass. It was 90 degrees with no humidity but felt like sticking your head in the oven. I saw no one over the age of forty. I witnessed two different groups playing soccer in the sand, with dust flying everywhere they ran.

Most groups making the trip for the first time were like me, looking to make a positive impact for the Nigerien people we would meet. Then we landed in one of the poorest countries in the world, and just the drive from the airport to the mission transformed me.

I was stunned by the amount of garbage on the roadsides. There was no trash pickup like in the US, so trash was discarded or gathered together and burned. We passed a motorcycle with three people riding—two on the seat and one on the handlebar. Another boy was riding a donkey. We stopped for traffic, and people knocked on the windows holding phone cards to sell or even Kleenex. Another man on a motorcycle was holding on to a goat across the seat as he steered between vehicles. It was full of dust and poverty like Bible times, but with motorized transportation.

Over the following days we visited orphanages and schools, and I was continually surprised by the joy I experienced in the people I met.

One of the best and worst moments of every mission trip is when we visit an orphanage, and the adults have all the children cleaned up and dressed up in their best clothes, then they march in and sing songs. It's a wonderful moment for the children, but it's also uncomfortable because we know that the adults have created the moment in an attempt to touch our hearts in a way that leads us to open our wallets. It can feel a bit like the kids are being used.

And yet the moment is so American. As a Chick-fil-A restaurant operator, I know as well as anybody the power of making emotional connections with our customers. We genuinely want our customers to be our friends, and we also want them to eat more chicken. The two go together.

We visited an orphanage that was home for about eighty children in Niamey. The children were all beautiful and healthy, and after they sang a few songs, the adults explained that we could sponsor a child for $860 per year. That amount would pay for food, clothing, and vaccinations. There were ten children who did not have sponsors.

We began each morning with devotions and prayers and ended each evening on the rooftop of the mission praying, worshiping, and processing our experiences of the day. I saw with my own eyes what Howe had described in the Christian schools—kids were learning, and their generation could transform the country if we could build more schools and provide more skilled teachers.

The first school we visited reflected the poverty I had quickly come to expect. Dust and dirt were everywhere, and the brooms to sweep the floors were nothing more than switches tied together. There were four kids to a desk.

Then we visited a school that had been built by French missionaries, and everything was tiled. Sinks in a lab looked like those I had grown up seeing in the United States. Outside, the space around the school was landscaped, and as we left, I said, "This is what we need to build."

Howe reminded me that this was not the US or Europe. We needed to understand and respect the culture here and not try to Americanize the village. Plus, we could build a lot more schoolrooms and teach a lot more kids if we spent less money on each school. This would be a positive tension in our discussions for several years.

Am I serving for what I can get or what I can give? As I left Niger, I was convinced that God was calling me to build schools in Niger, as many schools as I could. And I was committed to bringing as many people as possible to Niger to experience this place and these people. Maybe God would call others who came to a deeper commitment here too. Just as God called Peter onto the water, Howe had called me into the mission field of Niger, and I was about to invite anyone who would listen and answer the call.

I knew Haley would want to go more than anybody else in my life, and that possibility concerned me; I was scared. I had a restaurant to operate—soon to be two restaurants— and we had two young children. My bigger concern was, what if something happened to Haley? It just felt like the wrong time in our life for her to go on a trip like this, to a place that was now labeled a fourth-world country. If I am honest, I wasn't trusting the Lord with her protection and was questioning how I would raise two young kids and run a thriving business if, God forbid, something were to happen to her.

Back home, I told Haley about the need at the orphanage, and we decided to ask if there might be a boy about Hunter's age, seven. If we sponsored him, maybe they could be pen pals. The orphanage responded and sent us the photo of a boy named Rachid, who was eight. Haley and I became his sponsor.

Of course, Haley wanted to go on her own trip to Niger, and we didn't completely take the possibility off the table, despite my concerns. I prayed about it. But it wasn't until some close friends challenged me to trust God with Haley's safety that I began to find peace in the idea. If God was calling her to Niger, He would protect her. And if something happened to her on a trip that He called her to, then God would take care of us.

HUNTER: We had a picture of Rachid, and we knew our parents were helping him with school and clothes and stuff like that. Paulina and I were really young, and to me at that point, Rachid was just a picture. We sent him Christmas gifts, but I still understood it only at a surface level.

HALEY: I looked at that photograph of Rachid, and my compassion for him was deep. He lived in an orphanage. Where were his mother and father? Jason had described the poverty in Niger. So many destitute people. Did Rachid have any opportunity or hope? My hope was found in Jesus. Did Rachid know Jesus and how much He loves him? I felt a deep compassion for him and a desire to pour some of myself into him. To share my love. To help him stay healthy and to get an education if possible. To tell him about my Savior.

The photo was all we had to know him—an eight-year-old Nigerien boy with his front teeth chipped from a childhood accident on a slippery floor at the orphanage. What would become of him? I began to pray that the Lord would send me to meet this child and to be a picture of Jesus to him.

JASON: God lit a fire in me for the people of Niger, and I began to recruit others to go with me on a second trip in September 2008. I made sure we could visit the orphanage where Rachid lived so I could meet him. I took a few gifts and also a photo of Hunter and Paulina.

At the orphanage when we met, Rachid was very quiet. I sat down, and he sat in my lap. Then I showed him the picture, and he stared it for the longest time. The other adults in the group were playing games with the children while I attempted to connect with Rachid through the language and culture barriers. Then I glanced over at the light blue metal gate, which was the entrance to the orphanage, and about six to eight children from the surrounding village were peering around the gate. That was when it hit me: where else in the world could you go where kids from a village surrounding an orphanage have it so bad that they would rather live in the orphanage? Niger! Yes, this was an orphanage that Rachid and these children lived in, but at least they had a pastor and support staff who loved and cared for them. The surrounding village was the most impoverished of any place that I had ever seen, and it broke my heart.

HALEY: After Jason returned from his first mission, he felt confident that God would take care of me if I went to Niger. I immediately said, "Okay!" He didn't have to twist my arm.

Going to Africa was exactly what I wanted to do, and I signed up for a trip in November 2008. After scrolling through the pictures Jason had taken on his first mission, my heart was filled with excitement to experience this new culture and people group. After years of longing to serve on the mission field, my time was finally going to happen.

When friends began to ask where I was going, they thought I said, "Nigeria," because that was a place they had heard of. "No," I said. "It's Niger."

"Oh, who are you going with? What will you do there?"

I didn't know.

The more my friends asked, the more I realized how little I knew about this trip, this place, and these people. I was putting my trust in the Lord, yet fear began to creep in.

For most of my life, God had been telling me not to fear. When I was in sixth grade, I struggled academically. I had transferred to a private Christian school two years earlier, and the work was a challenge every day. My teacher, Diane Nelson, must have been aware, because one day she brought a Bible verse to me, Joshua 1:9: "Have I not commanded you? Be strong and courageous. Do not be afraid; do not be discouraged, for the LORD your God will be with you wherever you go."

"Haley," she said, "this verse reminds me of you, and I just want you to be encouraged by it. You know that the Lord is with you no matter what circumstances you go through."

That was a profound moment for me, realizing she was thinking of me in that way and that the Lord really would be with me. I'm not sure I understood the significance at the time, but I've continued to cling to that verse throughout my life.

As I grew older and people asked if I had a life verse, my first response was, "Well, I love the psalms, but Joshua 1:9 is the verse I live by."

When the Lord calls me out of my comfort zone in any capacity, my natural instinct, despite my life verse, is to be fearful. Yours too, probably. The Lord knows that, of course. Throughout the Bible, the Lord or His angels greet people with the words of Joshua 1:9: "Do not be afraid"—from Abraham to Moses to the prophets to the shepherds in the field after the birth of Christ. "Fear not!"

Yet when the Lord calls me to do something that I cannot do on my own, fear sets in. I don't feel confident or competent to accomplish the task. Then He commands me to be courageous. That's a command, not just an encouragement. "Have I not *commanded* you? Be strong and courageous."

He's telling me to step up to the thing He has called me to do.

"I am going to equip you," He says.

So, I carefully put one foot forward, and there He is, giving me hope and courage to take one more step.

JASON: While Haley was planning for her first trip to Niger, I was following up on my commitment to raise money to build schools there. My ideas gravitated toward sports events like a golf tournament and a road race. I reached out to Gary Stokan, who was president of the Chick-fil-A Bowl as well as the Atlanta Sports Council. He told me that with charity sports events, the key is to have enough participants to cover our costs. Then, all money from sponsorships would be profit. I told him I was intrigued by Howe Rice's success with the operators' dodgeball tournament in Richmond, and he said they had considered a dodgeball event in Atlanta. A popular movie in 2004, *Dodgeball: A True Underdog Story* had triggered interest in the sport across the country. The Atlanta Chick-fil-A operators agreed to sponsor a dodgeball tournament, and Gary's organization matched that amount. We had $50,000—an incredible start.

The logistics of the event were complex and far from a guaranteed success. We rented space in the Cobb Galleria convention center—expensive!—and we rented a net system to create sixteen courts in four quads. We designed posters for the Chick-fil-A Duck 'N' Dodge dodgeball tournament. We emphasized that we were raising money for schools in Niger, Africa, and more than 150 teams of six to ten players paid a $200 entry fee. In April 2008, seven months after my rooftop commitment to help raise money for schools in Niger, we had delivered!

We also made an unexpected connection. Don Whitney had founded a company that created sports-related corporate team-building events and also started the Labor Day US 10K Classic race in Cobb County. His son was on one of the dodgeball teams, and Don wanted to meet the organizers of the event. Don's kids also went to Whitefield Academy, so we had even more in common. Our connection would have a huge impact on our event's growth.

I do want to pause here and mention that not everyone was supportive of our efforts. Some believed that we should be doing more for our own community and not trying to raise money for those in another continent. Even close friends didn't quite understand or buy in to the vision. I always knew that opposition comes from the enemy, but I didn't realize it might also come from my friends. Remember, others may not have your perspective because God didn't speak to them. Press into God, do what He is calling you to do, and remember the support you need is the support God is giving you. If He called you to it, He will equip and empower you. God's calling and plans for your life will most likely be uncomfortable at times, but you will never experience deep satisfaction without stepping out of the boat.

HALEY: The weeks leading up to my first trip to Niger felt like the culmination of a lifetime of dreams and, maybe, the beginning of something even bigger than I anticipated. To call this trip a success, I needed to spend my time with God and realize His purpose for me. So many questions rolled around in my head and my heart, beginning with why I was going on this trip in the first place. What did He want me to do? How did He want me to change? Was He going to break my heart for Niger? What would that mean, and what would I do for Him in response?

Despite my confidence that God was guiding my steps, I had concerns about details. I didn't know anybody in the group I was traveling with. What would they be like? Would I bond with anyone? What would the food be like? Would there be air conditioning where we were staying? In the buses when we traveled?

I wrote these questions in my journal so I could carry them with me, and I reminded myself that I was fully confident that the Lord had called me to go on this mission with complete strangers to open my eyes to a part of the world I never imagined would change my life.

Jason had told me what to expect when I arrived in Niger, but I was not prepared for the reality of the poverty I saw. No matter how poor a person may be in the United States, there is some kind of assistance, from homeless shelters to government aid. Millions of people in Niger do not have this option. I asked the Lord what He would have me do in response to what I was seeing.

You can smell the poverty the moment you wake up in Niger. The odor isn't offensive. It's the smell of the ages, unlike anything you smell in the United States—of the earth and smoke from small pots being heated by an open fire, cooking foods you do not know, of livestock and camels and the dust they stir, of people who do not wear perfume or deodorant.

In the morning, we visited a clinic where mothers brought their malnourished babies. I had never seen a starving baby before I went to Africa; their tiny lethargic bodies made me weep. There was a line of hungry mothers carrying their malnourished children to the clinic where we were helping. The mothers nursed their babies, but their milk didn't produce enough nutrients because they weren't eating anything nutritious themselves. Exhausted from the miles they had walked to get to the clinic, it wasn't until they arrived that they realized their babies were so malnourished and weak that they could hardly move.

A volunteer laid a baby on a scale, and I began to cry again. The child was so tiny. They all were, and they were going to die without our help.

My tears were the only ones in the room. The mothers displayed no emotion as they handed their starving babies to be weighed. Some even looked at me as if to say, "Get it together, woman," and I was embarrassed to be so emotional. I took a deep breath and dried my eyes to make myself look strong, but after a while, I got comfortable with being who I was. I would allow the tears to stream, and I would wipe them and keep going.

I never believed the Nigerien women's dry eyes indicated a lack of caring for their children. It's just that death is so much closer to them every day. More than six babies die for every hundred births in Niger. That is ten times as many as in the US. Twenty years earlier, Niger's infant mortality rate had been twice that high. Clinics like these were an important part of saving those children, and a food product called Plumpy'Nut was working miracles.

It's a peanut-based food with powdered milk that's high-protein and adds weight quickly to malnourished infants. It was invented in 1996 by a French nutritionist, and it is so effective in preventing infant starvation, the Nigerien government controls distribution to prevent a black market. Our clinic was approved as a distribution site for the shelf-stable 3.25-ounce packets. Based on the age and weight of the babies, we gave each of the mothers two weeks' worth of Plumpy'Nut packs.

As the mothers came through, I couldn't help thinking of my two healthy children back home. These mothers and their children needed so much, and I felt honored that God allowed me to share His love in this way. I was also so thankful to be born in the United States where we have advanced medical care for our children when they are sick.

After my first full day of serving in Niger, the Lord affirmed what I had felt in my heart for so long: missions is what He created me to do. I remembered 2 John 1:6, which says, "And this is love: that we walk in obedience to his commands. As you have heard from the beginning, his command is that you walk in love."

I could think of no better way to show His love to the lost and least of these than serving on the mission field. But our time in Niger was short. With a full day of travel each direction, we had only five days in the country.

The day I looked forward to most was when we visited the orphanage where Rachid lived. I had looked at his picture countless times in the months since we had begun to sponsor him, and I had brought a bag full of clothes along with a toy and some candy for him.

We arrived at the orphanage, and I scanned every face in the room until I recognized him. Rachid stood out because, when he was very small, he had fallen and chipped both of his front teeth.

Once I spotted him, I eagerly grabbed a translator and hurried over to greet him. I wanted to hug him, as I always did my own children, but that's not something the Nigerien culture is used to. Hugging is not accustomed, especially between opposite sexes.

I gave Rachid his gifts, and after we talked for a while, I asked if he wanted to join me for a camel ride through his village. The directors of the orphanage had organized this fun event for our team and the children at the orphanage. Of course, I had never ridden a camel but was thrilled to be able to ask Rachid to ride with me.

"*Oui!*" he said, beaming. "*Oui!*"

Our translator took us to a camel owner, the camel knelt, and I climbed on, then Rachid climbed on with me. The camel smelled terrible, but we didn't care. We rode through the village strewn with trash, one of the poorest villages in Niamey, and although I was filled with joy to be making a memory with Rachid, my heart and mind were trying to process the extreme poverty all around us. Other Americans in our group took children from the orphanage for rides, and we became a camel parade through the village.

Afterward, we went back into the orphanage and played games with the children: hot potato, hopscotch, soccer, and basketball. We painted some of the girls' nails and blew bubbles with the toddlers. Even the teenaged children loved the bubbles—everybody loves bubbles!—and it became obvious that the children wanted our attention more than the toys we brought. The gift of time to just be with us, to laugh, to play, to be noticed, and to feel loved.

Then I heard children squealing outside. They were preparing for their favorite game, a water gun fight. The children versus the adults. It was clear they had plenty of experience with water gun fights, and their excitement was off the charts! We took our plastic water guns and learned how to refill, and we were reminded to keep our mouths closed because the water was not clean. The game must have gone for an hour or longer, until everybody was completely soaked.

Finally, as our time with the children grew short, my heart broke as I watched them laughing, playing, reaching for our hands just to be held or asking us to play just one more game with them. I wondered what happened in their hearts and minds as they watched us drive off and they waited for "another fun day" when the next team came. I wiped my eyes as the Holy Spirit reminded me these children were *His*. Psalm 146:9 says, "The LORD watches over the foreigner and sustains the fatherless and the widow." I had to trust that He would take care of them with our help.

My heart was full of so many mixed emotions. I once again grabbed a translator and said my goodbyes to Rachid. I was surprised at how attached I had become to him in just a few hours. We had just met! I couldn't wait to share with Jason and my children the amazing time I had at the orphanage with this beautiful boy.

That night before bed, I was praying, *Lord, please give me more time here. My whole life I've wanted to serve You in this way, talking to people who don't know Jesus. I want to stay longer!*

JASON: While Haley was gone, I realized how much work goes into taking care of the house and kids. I'd be lying if I didn't say I was counting the moments until she returned. It was hard but worth it to support the calling God placed on her life. Husbands, if your wife feels called by God to go overseas to further His kingdom, support her with enthusiasm. You and the kids will survive while she's gone. Her work could change both your lives forever, not to mention the many souls she could impact for eternity.

HALEY: On our last day, we packed up everything to go home. I was so grateful for the opportunity God had given me to serve in Niger and prayed that He would bring me back someday. I was trying to figure out when I would be able to return and see these people I had fallen in love with. My heart was filled with so much respect for the missionaries here who were serving full time. They were raising their children here, enduring power outages almost daily, contracting malaria and other sicknesses that aren't a risk in the United States. I asked them about things they missed from the US so that I could send those items with other teams. It was a small way that I could show love and do something for people who were giving up a life of comfort to serve the Lord and the people of Niger.

Our flight out left at midnight. Air France allowed us to check our tubs at the airport early, then we planned to go to LINK missionaries Brent and Shelley's home for dinner before boarding. At three in the afternoon, we loaded up and drove to the airport. When we got out of the van, Brent was already in the terminal. His shoulders had dropped, and he was clearly upset about something.

"There's a problem," he said. "The Air France agent says a flock of geese flew into the plane, and some of them got sucked into the engines. Air France won't be able to make the repairs for two days. You all are stuck in Niger, but we will figure out a plan."

My heart leaped for joy, but many others were upset and crying as they called home to share the news. When it was my turn to call home, I was afraid of what Jason's response would be. He had been at home with two small children, trying to run his businesses for a week with little help. It was 9:00 a.m. in Atlanta, so the restaurant was still busy with the breakfast rush.

JASON: I was not happy. In fact, the first words *in my mind* were, "See! This is why you don't go in the first place. Things happen!" But I stopped myself before saying those words out loud, or maybe the Holy Spirit stopped me, despite my selfish mindset.

It didn't take long for me to realize I was going to have to check my attitude. Haley had a true heart for reaching God's children across the world. If He wanted Haley to serve Him in this way, I would have to get out of the way and let her serve. Haley had stepped out of the boat. Who was I to ask her to sit back down?

HALEY: The Lord is faithful when we step out in obedience to what He calls us to. During this mission, the Lord blessed me with several new friends. Jason had met one of these ladies on his first mission and had asked her if she would look after me on this mission. The Lord knew I needed these ladies in my life, and to this day Debbie and Sharon are two of my closest friends. Debbie was one of my roommates on this first mission. She and Sharon were able to explain and educate me on many differences between American and Nigerien cultures. They were also there when I met Rachid for the first time, a moment forever etched in our hearts as friends.

I was so thankful the Lord had allowed me the privilege of seeing the Nigerien people the way He sees them—to share His love and light in this area of the world that needs to know who Jesus is and how much He loves them. Until next time, I was praying, *What's next Lord? When will I be able to return? How can I help these people from halfway across the world? Will anyone understand or have a passion to go with me?*

After I returned home and began to share stories of my time in Niger with friends and family, their next question was, "When are you going back?" They could feel my passion and excitement for this work. I began to pray and ask the Lord for a chance to return, and the Lord answered that prayer and called me to serve on two medical teams. But I knew I couldn't go back without building a support structure for Jason and our children so they could all do their best at work and at school.

JASON: Haley took charge. She knew she would be going back, and she knew I would need help, so she asked some of her friends to help with the kids, taking them to school and picking them up in the afternoon. They even brought us meals, so I didn't have to come home from work early to fix dinner. My mom and dad helped too.

The times when Haley was in Africa became special times for me to spend with our kids, because she had arranged for everything, including great food, and she was serving the Lord.

PAULINA: When one of my parents was away, that was always difficult. I knew that it was good and that they were doing good things. I knew that when they came back, they would have a gift for me, and as a kid I was excited for that. But there was also this tension when my mom was away. My dad would struggle to pull it all together for us to get the meals from people and to take us to school and practice. A part of me was thinking, *This is hard*.

When my dad would leave, it just felt empty in the house without our protector there. Hunter had to step up and take on most of that role. I never felt like the mom when my mother was away, although after the boys moved out, there were a couple of times when she left and it was just me and my dad. I felt a responsibility to help and take care of him, even though he was still the one pulling meals together. It just always seemed very different. I could tell he missed her, and I felt lonely because I was alone most of the time. Looking back now, I am so thankful for these times. My parents were modeling for me what it was to step out in faith. They did what God called them to do, and I am doing the same by attending Colorado Christian University and getting a degree in global studies to join the mission field.

JASON: In the meantime, we were raising more money for schools in Niger and planning for our second dodgeball tournament in 2009. We had already outgrown the Galleria, and we moved to the Atlanta Silverbacks outdoor soccer stadium.

One day at a Panera Bread, I paid the cashier and noticed a collection-type box on the counter for a local charity. There was a lot of change in the box. In that moment, God spoke to me and said, "You can do that." I got with my assistant, and we looked online and found clear plastic boxes that look like small homes—or a schoolhouse! We ordered them and created stickers for them that read: Give change to create change!

We created a Schools for Niger, Africa (SFNA) brochure and had thousands printed. Soon we had more than twenty Chick-fil-A restaurants with schoolhouse cash boxes on their counters collecting loose change from guests.

You won't believe this, but we raised about $25,000 a year in loose change. I noticed that box in Panera, God spoke to me, and I got to work.

In Niger, the money we raised was accelerating the construction of new classrooms. Building schools there is very different than what is done in the States. They obtain the land and build one or two classrooms, fill them with kinder-garten and first-grade students, and then the following year build more classrooms. The classroom and campus grow with the growth of the students. This process allowed us to invest a little at a time and help more than one school.

The classrooms we funded were constructed with hand-made cinder blocks, and the finished product was a very simple structure. The blocks or bricks were made on site and allowed to dry in the dessert sun. You would think this would make the process easier, since they build the materials on site. But it's not so. The challenge is the lack of a running water source to mix concrete for the blocks.

I had seen Nigerien men hauling water in five-gallon jugs from far away just to make the concrete blocks, and I asked for an estimate for digging a well for the school. I texted the SFNA board asking for their approval. This well would help with the building materials immediately, but in the long run it would be a water supply for the school students and the surrounding community. The hope is if we are good neighbors and share the water with those in the village, then they may ask, Who is this Jesus you all talk about?

FOUR

CALLED OUT OF A FLOOD TO OPEN THE EYES OF THE BLIND

HALEY: Jason and I often use the word *biblical* to describe our experiences in Niger. The heat, the dust, the animals walking on the main roads, and the poverty create pictures you might imagine of New Testament Palestine. Then we see God working in that place, and the experience feels like we're living in the ancient pages ourselves. But in 2009, *biblical* could have described the week *before* I made my second trip to Niger.

My friend Kristi Collett lives on eight acres with six horses plus goats, pigs, chickens, turkeys, and various animals that somebody else had thought might be a good idea to bring home, then decided otherwise. "People realize they don't really want a pig in their house," Kristi says, "and then what?"

Then they give the pig to Kristi, and she takes care of it. Her barn is way bigger than her house.

The animals are not all for fun. Kristi is a professional. She teaches horseback riding lessons, has a barrel racing arena that she built on her property, and occasionally leads trail rides. She hosts birthday parties and kids' camps, and she sells eggs from her chickens.

I met her when she was in the first BSF group I ever led. We both laugh now about how she never returned my phone calls. As the group leader, I called every member of our group every week to find out what they might be struggling with or to ask if they had any prayer requests. Every week I left a message on Kristi's phone, and every week she didn't call back. After a while it started to hurt my feelings. I like to make connections. Years later Kristi told me she was trying to be respectful of my time. "You were a mom with small kids, and you had so many responsibilities," she said. "I thought I was being helpful by not calling you back."

In class on Wednesdays, it was obvious Kristi was digging deeply into the lesson every week. She always came with thoughtful questions and comments. But between Wednesdays, we were not in touch, so we didn't become friends until she was out of my group and became a leader herself.

Kristi was the first person I recruited for a trip to Niger. When I say, "I recruited," I have to say that it's God who calls us to make a trip like that. They're making a bigger commitment to God than they would ever make to me. They're committing themselves to Jesus and His children.

The group included several medical professionals, and we were going to provide health-care services for two weeks in Niger. Kristi and I were assigned to the eye-care team. This intrigued me because I had worn glasses since I was a little girl. A few weeks before our trip, we flew to North Carolina, where an optometrist trained us to use a handheld refractor and high school algebra to determine the correct prescription for someone needing glasses. It sounds unsophisticated, but the people we were serving had no other opportunity to have their vision tested. In their poverty, they could not pay for an eye exam, much less for glasses. Our team would be taking used glasses that had been donated to Lions Clubs and other organizations.

Then the rain started to fall in Atlanta. Torrential downpours day after day. Four days before we were to leave Atlanta, the local newspaper showed photos of the Great American Scream Machine at Six Flags under water. The Scream

Machine was the highest roller coaster in the world, and it was mostly submerged after more than a week of constant downpours. That's how much it had rained that September in Atlanta.

A few miles northwest of Six Flags, Kristi was taking care of her animals and keeping them in the barn. On the first few days of rain, everything was fine. A small creek across Kristi's property would rise and fall as the rain came and went. On Sunday, September 20, it rained hard all night. More than twenty inches of rain near Kristi's house—a record rainfall—turned the creek into a lake. At dawn on Monday, the water was ankle deep in the yard, and rain kept pouring down. Then, in a thirty-minute span, water rose to her porch and was at her doorstep.

She moved a few things around in the house as the water continued rising, and then she hurried to the barn, where the water was waist deep and still rising. There she was met by the pig swimming toward the door. She put her hands gently on him and guided him out to a place where he could put his feet down and walk to higher ground. The horses were nervous in their stalls, and in the rising water Kristi had a hard time opening the door to her horse Pistol's stall. When she finally got it open, she couldn't coax Pistol to come out. She went to the tack room for bridles, but the high water had lifted them just enough to slip off their hooks and sink to the floor. She bent down under water and felt around until she found them, swam back to Pistol, and put the bridle on him. She talked gently to him and kept him calm, and she was able to lead him out of his stall, through the water in the barn, and up to higher ground. The other horses, maybe because they had seen Pistol, let Kristi lead them out one by one.

Kristi called and told me about her horses, and I thought about the times when Jesus has asked me to trust Him— when I trust Him, He calms me and leads me to safety.

At 3:40 on Monday afternoon, she texted me telling me her house and barn were flooded. I called the team leader for our trip, and I was crying. I asked her to pray for Kristi. Then I started calling our BSF friends. Hunter and Paulina were out of school because of the flooding, so we headed toward Kristi's to help. I called Jason at the restaurant, then stopped by my friend Julie's house to drop off some Whitefield Parent Association items. She, Brian, and Patrick wanted to help too. Jason sent out an email to friends, and Nicole, Cassidy, and Brad Roper responded and headed over to Kristi's.

Roads and bridges were flooded between our house and Kristi's, and we had to make several detours getting there. By the time we arrived, water was actually receding, but it was leaving behind a disaster. It had risen to her windowsills, and inside there was enough water to float her refrigerator and tip it over.

Kristi was confused deep in her spirit. She knew God had called her to the mission trip, but there was no way she could leave now. Our flight was just two days away. With water all around her, all she could think about was cleaning up. If she let it sit wet for ten days while she was in Niger, the house would be ruined.

From the road, more cars came down the driveway to the edge of the water, and more people got out and waded in. By midafternoon, the water had dropped below the floor, and thirty people were taking out furniture and things that could not be salvaged. The floor looked like a muddy creek bed.

Kristi didn't know a lot of the people cleaning out her house. Afterward, she would tell others that Jason and I were the connection between them and her. But Christ was the connection. Each of the people helping felt His love and shared His love with a child of God who needed help.

We had been working for seven hours, and I cried when Kristi told me she wouldn't be able to go to Niger, but I understood. I was also determined that she was going. Satan would not win this battle.

"What if we could get everything cleaned up in time?" I asked. I knew it was crazy, but I couldn't give up hope.

"Maybe," Kristi said looking around at the mud.

On Tuesday morning, everybody was back. Water had receded completely from the house, and the real cleanup could begin. We were all on our hands and knees with buckets and brushes and bleach cleaning one square foot at a time. We loaded a truck with a ruined mattress, sofa, rugs, and linens and took them to the dump. Jason had gotten a bunch of big fans to dry the house faster.

By the end of the day on Tuesday, Kristi's house had been transformed, with floors clean and fans blowing. There was still much to be done, but Jason, Cheryl, and others told Kristi they would keep working while she went to Niger.

"I guess I can go, then," she said. At that point we were all exhausted, and there was still so much more to be done. The cars returned on Wednesday, and Kristi worked alongside everybody until we had to leave for the airport in the afternoon. We boarded the plane for the flight, and when we took off, the emotions finally caught up with Kristi.

"Sitting on the plane, I felt this deep humility," she said later. "Never in my life had I needed so much from other people. It was like I saw a picture of the body of Christ I had read about and talked about but had never experienced personally like that. I was overwhelmed with gratitude and humility. People I didn't even know had been working at my house and were still working at my house on their hands and knees for me, a stranger. Would I have done that for them?"

In fact, Kristi was on her way to Niger to do just that—to help strangers half a world away.

She sat beside me and opened her carry-on bag. She pulled out the journal she had received in advance of the trip and opened it to a question: What are your expectations for your trip? She smiled and wondered what possible expectation she could have. Somewhere in the inner recesses of her mind, she might find some expectations and bring them forward, but at that moment she was exhausted and emotionally spent. The plane flew into the night over the Atlantic Ocean, and she closed her eyes.

We began our descent to Paris, the first leg of the trip, on Thursday morning, and Kristi felt pain in her ears, a little more than she was used to with the change in altitude. Over the next few minutes, her pain level rose from 1 to 10, like her head was going to explode; she was crying in pain. She had developed an ear infection from the water in the barn, and the pain was almost unbearable. We landed, and I asked one of the doctors traveling with us if he would help, but all of his medicines were in the luggage underneath the plane. Kristi would have to endure the next flight, from Paris to Niamey, Niger, before she could get relief.

Approaching Niamey, one by one the women went back to the bathroom and changed out of jeans and into long skirts, which is expected in Nigerien culture. Kristi bore the pain as we descended. We landed and taxied to a stop, and the ground crew rolled a stairway over to the plane and opened the door. Heat like I had experienced only one other time—my first trip to Niger—poured into the cabin and immediately overwhelmed the plane's air conditioning. The temperature outside was over 100 degrees, and heat radiating up from the asphalt tarmac was way hotter than that.

"Feels like we're Hansel and Gretel," Kristi said, "about to be cooked in a little oven."

She must have been wondering what she had gotten herself into. Flood, ear infection, and now this incredible heat. At least her pain subsided after the doctor gave her antibiotics.

Later in the week, Kristi and I were both a little nervous and excited to be able to help with the training we had received back in the States. A long line of people hoping to get eyeglasses formed.

The team had brought boxes and boxes of glasses, hundreds of pairs organized by prescription strength. We didn't have as many children's glasses, though. Just one tiny pair with Coke-bottle lenses, and I wondered about that poor child's near blindness.

Matching people to glasses was going to be more complicated than picking up readers from Walmart. With each person, we used the handheld refractor and went through the same routine our own eye doctors use. We taped an eye chart to a folding chair twenty feet away and had each person look through the refractor. With a translator alongside, I asked as I switched lenses in the refractor, "Which is clearer, one or two?"

Then I'd change the lenses again. "One or two?"

After a few minutes, we had the prescription narrowed down for each eye. Kristi worked the "fitting room" and looked for a pair of glasses that matched the prescription. We had an assembly line going, serving as many people as possible.

With some of the older people who had cataracts, we did the best we could with the strongest glasses we had, and they were so grateful to be able to see a little bit better. The men would walk away stoically, and the women would sometimes squeal with delight. I even received a few hugs from women who were overjoyed by the gift of sight they had been given! My heart longed for them to also receive spiritual sight.

Near the end of the day, a little girl with braids and beads in her hair came in with her mother, and she could hardly see at all. With the refractor, it was obvious she was guessing when I asked which was clearer. I thought I had it right, and Kristi took a pair of children's glasses from the box. She put them on, and when she looked at the chart, she was still guessing. She wanted to see so badly, I began to pray, "Lord please help me. This is not my area of expertise. Give me wisdom."

Kristi scanned the glasses and their prescriptions again and then she walked over and handed the precious little girl the Coke-bottle glasses. She put them on, and she smiled. I still wasn't sure she was seeing, so I asked her to turn around, and I placed a coin on the ground behind her. She turned back and walked straight over and picked up the coin. She could see! I picked her up and she wrapped her arms around me, and my heart was overflowing with gratitude. My Savior heard my prayer and provided the exact pair of glasses this child needed. It was miraculous!

> The Spirit of the Lord is on me, because he has anointed me to proclaim good news to the poor. He has sent me to proclaim freedom for the prisoners and recovery of sight for the blind, to set the oppressed free. (Luke 4:18)

I thought about the stories in the Bible in which Jesus healed blind people. We had brought to Africa little glasses that an American child had outgrown, and through them a Nigerien child received the miracle of sight.

Our translators were local Christian pastors, and they would share the gospel and invite each person to their church. We wanted each of them to know that we were sharing the love of Jesus Christ along with the gift of improved vision.

There were three others on the eye-care team, and we kept up a crazy pace; we saw more than two hundred patients a day for six days. We were working twelve hours every day, with people standing in line for hours to see us. By the end of the week, we had seen 1,300 patients.

While on these medical missions, I was embarrassed to find myself in a puddle of tears yet again. I felt people looking at me and wondering, *Why is she crying again?* I am a very compassionate person who loves deeply, so when I see the "least of these" suffering, tears come naturally. It is one of the few times in my life where I was praying, *Lord, help me be strong and not cry.* Joshua 1:9 popped into my mind over and over during my time on this medical mission, and I always felt more comfortable when I was in a smaller group of just women.

This mission stirred up so many emotions within me. To see with my own eyes children suffering with open wounds that looked like leprosy, babies that were on death's door from malnourishment, elders who could no longer see due to cataracts, babies burning up with fever due to malaria, and so many diseases that would easily be treated in the US—why was I blessed to be born in the United States? This poverty that we were witnessing was heart-wrenching, yet God had brought us here to love these people and to share the good news of who He is and how they could have hope of eternal life in Him.

I was amazed at how you may not be able to speak the same language as another person but you can still communicate love to them through your actions, hugs, and smiles. Love knows no boundaries or languages. My time spent serving on this medical mission were some of the hardest days I had ever experienced, yet they were the most profound because the Lord had met us in these hard places and equipped us to do what He had called us to. When we follow Him there will always be sacrifices made, but that is where sanctification takes place and we become more like our Savior!

When we boarded the plane for home, we were exhausted, and my tears once again began to fall. My heart was heavy with all that we had seen and experienced on this mission, trying to process the poverty, pain, and harsh living conditions these precious people endure daily. My mind was racing, wondering when I would be able to return to this place that had stolen my heart. Thankfully, Kristi's ear infection was cured, and she flew home pain free to a dry, clean house and memories that we both would treasure in our hearts forever.

FIVE

CALLED TO LEAD AND PREACH THE WORD

HALEY: After I returned home from my second medical mission, I once again began to pray, "Lord, what is next?" I looked at photos from my trip, reflected on my time in Niger, and was taken back to those moments when I experienced God's presence. Then the idea popped into my head, *What if I could lead my own team to Niger?* This would truly be stepping out of the boat. I would be able to determine the length of the mission, which would allow us to serve longer, and I could invite all women. I know that I'm more willing to share my emotions with a group of all women than with a mixed group, and I believe others are too. Simply put, I'm not as embarrassed when I cry with other women. I also knew a team of women would be more interested in serving women and children, and I felt this was my calling. I asked LINK about the possibility, and they encouraged me. Little did I know that would be the Lord's plan for me for the next ten years!

LINK put me on the schedule for a group in October 2011. Jason had put together his team for January 2011, and nine months later I would be leading the first women's LINK team to this area of Niger. I began praying and asking the Lord who I should ask to join me on this adventure. After all, this was His team. Leading for the first time, I wanted to step out of the way to ensure that the people who went on this mission were the ladies God had called to go. I was smart enough to know that if people joined me on this mission and they were not who God had planned, things could go terribly wrong. So, with a pure heart I honestly sought the Lord and surrendered to His will and waited for Him to give me names of ladies to ask.

As He revealed names to me, I began asking them, and one *yes* after another started building my faith and excitement that the Lord would provide each lady He had purposed to be a part of this mission.

In the meantime, Jason's next team was scheduled to meet and leave from the Chick-fil-A headquarters' parking

CALLED TO LEAD AND PREACH THE WORD | 103

deck, and several of the operators' wives came along to see them off. After saying our goodbyes and praying over the team, we stayed to visit in the parking deck. Phil Nichols's wife, Kelli, was there, and I had felt God nudging me to ask her to join our women's team. I didn't know Kelli well, yet it felt clear to me that God wanted me to invite her. I mentioned the possibility to her and asked her to pray about it to see if God was calling her as well.

Kelli was polite but didn't commit. She tells what happened next, after Jason's group came back from their trip to Niger and Phil told her what he had seen:

> I had seen Phil cry at our wedding and when our kids were born but not much since. He isn't usually very emotional. After coming home from Niger, it was like his world had been rocked. He had seen one of the poorest countries in the world but also experienced all of what God was doing there. I knew to fully understand how Phil felt, I needed to go too. God opened doors for me to be able to go with Haley the following year.

Kelli called and told me she was in.

I called Jason's cousin, Cara, who lived in Kentucky, and invited her to join our team. Jason and Cara are close, and when she had visited us in recent years, she had listened intently to our stories of Niger, especially my experiences with malnourished children and Plumpy'Nut. She had not grown up in church and didn't connect with the spiritual aspect of our mission, but she was up for an adventure and an opportunity to help.

I had two meetings with my team members to prepare all of us for the trip. Most everybody on the trip takes a leadership role. We have a hydration leader to make sure everybody is drinking water all day. We have a wake-up leader, a breakfast leader, and a devotional leader who all make sure the day starts right. Every leader has a checklist, and we're super organized so that when we're on the ground in Niger, we can make the most of our time. Jason and a few others helped me pack our tubs of supplies ahead of time, and I was ready to go.

Then, forty-eight hours before we were scheduled to leave, the director, Rodrigo, called and said, "Haley, I have some bad news. The team that's here in front of you has decided to stay longer, and that's going to overlap with your mission. So, we're not going to have room for you at the Bible school. You're going to have to stay at a hotel."

My mind instantly started reeling, thinking, *You've got to be kidding me! I won't have meeting space for the team to gather every evening. I won't have space for the supplies and tubs we're bringing and no freezer to store water bottles.*

Every system I had in place for my team would not be an option at this hotel. How could they do this to me? My first time leading and I'm thrown to the wolves! We would have to create a new itinerary for every day of the trip. What about security? Food? Everything went out the window. Would anybody else be staying with us? I suddenly felt very alone. I prayed, *God, I know You are allowing this for a reason, and I just have to trust You.*

The Lord reminded me once again that there are no surprises with God, and He knew this was the plan before I was ever born. I knew from Scripture that He would never leave me or forsake me, so I began to process the information I had been given and pray for the Lord's wisdom as I navigated this new road. I wish I could say my prayers gave me complete peace.

Our mission trips to Niger run smoothly because we and other teams follow a process that we've worked out over dozens of visits. The simplest things we take for granted here are part of the process there, and everything centered on the Bible school where we stayed. The missionaries prepared our meals. We could use the refrigerator and freezer. We had access to bottled water we could trust was clean. No group had ever stayed at the hotel, so we would be creating processes on the fly.

We arrived, and our accommodations were more like air-conditioned huts. Most of the women were making their first trip to Niger, and I had wanted it to be perfect. Instead, I had to surrender more to God and make the best of a situation that would be impossible to make smooth and systematic. Day by day, we were having to be flexible with meals, transportation, and organization. This was not at all how I envisioned leading my first team.

This mission had plenty of challenges: air conditioning went out in one of the huts and those ladies had to bunk with us on the floor anywhere we could fit them. One traveler took a sleeping aid and didn't allow enough time for it to wear off, so when we went through security at the Paris airport, she got pulled in the back to be screened and almost missed the flight back to Atlanta. Yet we persevered, we learned to be flexible, and we learned that God's plans are the best plans. The mission was amazing, and we were able to serve in many wonderful places and share the gospel with many women and children. We returned home with full hearts and closer to the Lord because of our time spent serving in Niger.

As I prayed once again about who I should ask to join me for the upcoming mission, Cara and Kelli eagerly agreed to go back. I continued to pray, and one after another the Lord brought together a group of nine ladies. Kelli had recruited a few ladies who were new and excited. We were able to visit some schools, day cares, orphanages, and the national hospital; we were able to ride camels and take a "boat ride" to see hippos. As a group I would pray aloud before heading out for the day, and others would volunteer as well.

After several days of praying, I was concerned that Cara did not feel comfortable with a group of Christian women praying out loud almost all the time. She was uncharacteristically quiet at times, and I wanted to be sensitive to her. Then she got food poisoning, and she had to stay behind with the missionaries while the team went on a search for hippos in the Niger River. She told me later that lying alone in her room, so far from home, she thought about what she had seen since she arrived—goats and cows eating garbage to survive; people eating those goats to survive. How nutritious was that? She wondered what she could do to help in a country that didn't even pick up the garbage. After many prayers from Cara and the team, she was back on her feet the next day.

Each year there were always special memories from each mission and miracles of the Lord's hand at work. The wives of Christian pastors in Niger pour themselves out so much, supporting their husbands and the people in their churches. The leadership at LINK asked if we would host a conference for the wives so they could be poured into. I loved that idea, and so did the women with me on the trip. We began to map out the day, with one speaker in the morning and another in the afternoon. I told them they could share their testimony or whatever God laid on their hearts. We also had time for games and lunch, and time to spend just getting to know one another.

We held our first women's conference at the LINK Outreach Center. The LOC had an outdoor area where we could play games and a thatch-covered area where we could sit away from the blazing sun and talk about the gospel. The testimonies were moving for everybody, but our play time created the most lasting memories.

I asked Kelli to be in charge of games. She can be very creative and is willing to try things I might never consider—games you would think no adult would play, like a balloon relay. Kelli knew intuitively that the women of Niger would enjoy them. The women had to blow up a balloon, then run to the finish line and sit on it until it burst. They were running with babies on their backs, and then bouncing on their balloons until they popped. They laughed and laughed. But that was nothing compared to Duck, Duck, Goose, or *Canard, Canard, Oie*. The women were so competitive. When you touched a woman's back and then started around the circle, you'd better run fast. Kelli tried to outrun a woman who grabbed her skirt and almost pulled it off. We had to remind them, "No tripping!"

These women had come to the conference dressed to the nines, with makeup and their best skirts and head wraps on. By the time we finished the games, they were sweating and their makeup was running, and we were all so comfortable with each other. With her games, Kelli had helped create an environment of fun and sharing. We wanted to share our love and give them a time to completely relax.

At the end of the day, we asked each of them to sit in a chair and take off their sandals so we could wash their feet. The fifty or so women were reluctant, but we gently persuaded them and let them know we wanted to serve them. As pastors' wives, these women are always pouring into others, so it was a challenge for them to be served.

This was one of the most powerful moments I have experienced in Niger. With our soapy hands, we could feel the thick calluses from a lifetime of walking in this hot, dusty land. To me, it felt truly biblical. The lives of ancient Hebrews were not so different from these twenty-first-century Nigerien women. We rubbed softly at first, then more firmly as the women relaxed and allowed us to massage the soles of their feet. We read Scripture and explained that we were modeling one of the final acts of Jesus, serving and loving these beautiful women.

When we finished with each woman, we invited her to another pair from our group who then painted her toenails or fingernails. Then we gave each of them a drawstring bag with soap, shampoo, conditioner, and lotion. One of our prayers was that each woman would go home that day feeling like a beautiful daughter of God.

Not every encounter was so peaceful, however. One day, we were hurrying to the baby center, and Edouard, our translator, was nervous. The woman who ran the center was a stickler. She kept a tight schedule, and if we were a little bit tardy, she wouldn't be happy.

His phone rang, and it was her. "*Où es-tu?*" "Where are you?"

Edouard told her we were close. She said she had another appointment, and we should hurry, because she didn't have much time.

Edouard hung up and told us what she had said.

"Okay," I said to the group, "our number one goal is to reflect Jesus to this lady. Let her know we love her."

We arrived, and the director was not smiling, but we were. She showed us around the center, and we asked questions. We could tell right away that she wanted more than smiles. She wanted respect. And we did respect her. I had told my group about the struggle to keep malnourished infants alive and how Plumpy'Nut was literally a life saver.

We saw again, firsthand, the tiny, tiny babies struggling to live, and our smiles turned to tears. There were at least two babies in each bed, some of them with flies crawling on their faces. We held these precious babies in our arms and would pray over them that one day they would come to know Jesus. We also provided reusable diapers for the babies that had been donated by many friends and family back in the US.

It was time for us to leave, and the women struggled to lay the babies back down in these cribs with bugs crawling in the bed. The harsh reality was that the workers were doing their best, but the babies were not receiving the care they truly needed.

The director extended our visit, to the point that she was late for her next appointment, because she felt the connection too. I hugged her when it was time to leave, and she hugged me back. She was Muslim, and we were Christian, and I believe she saw the kindness and love of Jesus we had shown to her.

Christian church in Niger lasts about three hours on most Sundays, with announcements, singing, and over an hour of worship. And worship is a glorious sight. In Nigerien society, women are not supposed to speak often. It's a male-dominated culture. But on Sunday, in church, nobody holds the women back when they're praising God. They dress up in bright African prints—long, flowing skirts—and they'll get up and dance in the aisles. The Bible writes about David dancing before the Lord with all his heart; well, that's what these women were doing. They were pouring out their hearts to the Lord without concern for what anyone thought. Their worship is loud and heartfelt.

The men also dress in their Sunday best, with clean dress shirts and nice shoes. When we're there, they sometimes go even longer than three hours because they ask someone from our group to preach. Church in Niger was so different from anything I had ever experienced in America. It challenged me to truly assess my worship for my King! Was I ashamed of what others may think if I wanted to raise my hands and no one else did? The Africans taught me that worship is a way of honoring my King. I joined in with the "train of ladies" that danced their way all around the church that day. I always share with my new travelers that after they attend a traditional African church service they will worship differently. Attending church in Niger was a small picture of what I imagine heaven will be like. Different cultures, different colored skin, different languages, all worshipping one Savior!

JASON: In January 2012, Phil Nichols and I were on the streets handing out copies of the *Book of Hope*—a Christian pamphlet about Jesus and personal hygiene—when a man began yelling at us. We turned to face him, and he came toward us and literally got in my face, yelling in French and clearly agitated. We stood in the orange, sandy streets as sweat began to run down our backs and foreheads; I wasn't sure if it was from the temperature outside or because this interaction was clearly heating up.

It was important to me that we let this man know that we were good people sharing the love of Jesus, so instead of shutting up or leaving, as he obviously wanted us to do, I continued to calmly speak God's Word. Neither of us knew the other's language, but I knew what he was saying as clearly as he understood me. I opened the book and showed him pictures of Jesus and spoke of God's love. Then he snatched the book from my hand and ripped it apart.

I've seen local missionaries have these encounters many times, and they've never ended in violence. Niger is generally not a violent country. There are almost no guns, and I haven't witnessed any fistfights. After a few more minutes, it was clear the man was not going to stop yelling, so I wished him peace and we walked away. I was not afraid. But a few minutes later, Phil told me he couldn't remember a time when he'd been that shook up, worried for our safety.

"Really?" I said, realizing maybe I was not taking the threats we faced seriously enough.

That night as our group was on the rooftop reflecting on the day, I knew that God had called me to this place to speak His Word. I also knew that He sees our lives like a parade—He can see the beginning and the end, and if it's my time to go, then what better way to go than serving the Lord.

I should not be foolish, but I'm confident that the Lord is with us. I believe I was supposed to be preaching to that man at that time. God had a divine appointment with him, and He was using me.

Of course, my hope was for the man to accept Christ. That did not happen, but God revealed Himself to me through the encounter on a sandy street with the *Book of Hope* in my hand.

John Piper, the respected pastor, clarifies how love compels followers of Jesus to share Jesus: "Don't wait for a feeling or love in order to share Christ with a stranger. You already love your heavenly Father, and you know that this stranger is created by Him, but separated from Him ... so take those first steps in evangelism because you love God. It is not primarily out of compassion for humanity that we share our faith or pray for the lost; it is first of all, love for God."[5]

The heat in Niger presses down on you during the day, and the streets get hotter and hotter. You don't see many people out and about. But late in the afternoon, they start moving, and by the time the sun sets, they've set up a row of little shops, if you can call them that. They're more like cubbies where they might sell bananas or other fruit or a shirt or a skirt. There's even a little pharmacy, where the top seller is Kleenex because of the constant dust. The markets stay open until one or two in the morning because it's so much cooler that time of day.

One year I helped lead a youth team, and as we were driving around, they were watching the camels and the donkeys make their way along the paved roads just as any motorcycle or car would do. In addition to the animals, we would see "walking pharmacies," men with what seemed like small drugstores attached to their backs, and men selling phone cards or sandals. Then I saw a guy carrying a big wooden board with dozens of pairs of sunglasses on it, and I felt a prompting to stop our driver and let everybody off to buy a pair. But caution or something got the better of me, and I didn't speak up. Later, I regretted missing the opportunity.

Author Mark Batterson says, "Our ultimate destiny is determined by whether or not we seize the God-ordained opportunities presented to us. If we seize those opportunities, the dominos continue to fall and create a chain reaction. But if we miss those opportunities, we short-circuit God's plan for our lives."[6]

A year later I had a group of adult men with me on another mission, and as we drove through Niger, I saw another guy carrying the same kind of board filled with sunglasses. We weren't in Niamey, and it's not quite as safe outside the city, but my heart leapt, and I yelled, "Stop!"

Our driver hit the brakes, and I explained to the guys, "Here's what we're going to do. We're going to get out of the van, and everybody picks out a pair of sunglasses. Then I'll pay for it, and we take our picture with the guy. Then we tell him Jesus loves him, hop back in the van, and we're on our way."

My co-leader on the trip, Brad, is a Chick-fil-A operator, and he's very conservative. He said, "I'm not sure this is in the handbook. I'm not sure we should be . . ."

"But this will be fun! And we will bless him with some sales." I interrupted. You see, opportunities are a gift from God. What we choose to do with these opportunities is our gift to God.

So the driver stopped the van and we all jumped out and picked out our sunglasses, and I began to tell him about Jesus.

Then Edem, our translator, stepped in and started witnessing with real passion.

A crowd of men began to gather around us, loud and harsh, demanding that we stop talking to the man. They told the man to stop listening to Edem, but Edem kept on, and the man kept listening, and he accepted Christ right there on the side of the road. Edem got his cell phone number so he could follow up, and then we all gathered around him and had our picture taken. We prayed over him out loud, and then we hustled onto the van and left, but Edem stayed in touch with the "Sunglasses Christian."

Later that night, when we gathered on the roof of the LOC to discuss the highs and lows of the day, that was definitely our high. One man in our group, Bryan, had been quiet most of the time. He's a big guy, nicknamed "Big Vision," who has been with me several times to Niger, and he said our high was actually his low. That moment on the side of the road had made him extremely nervous for our safety, and he had stood back and watched the crowd for anybody who might commit violence against us. As much as we were responding to God's call, so was Bryan. The moment could have gone badly, but God had us.

I keep those sunglasses and the photo on my desk as a reminder of an incredible moment when we were bold and God acted, and also as a reminder that God protects us, sometimes by giving us earthly protectors.

We should recognize the opportunities when God calls us out of the boat, and we need to be ready to say yes. Sitting there watching the world go by from the van should not be an option when you are living for Jesus.

HALEY: A lot of people don't feel comfortable traveling from the United States to Niger because the country is 94 percent Muslim. When they hear "Muslim," they think, *Muslim extremist*. But that's not the case. The people are welcoming when they see Americans because they know we're not coming for a vacation. We're there to help them in some capacity. The culture is friendly and, for the most part, happy. We see people laughing and dancing just walking down the road, even in poverty we can't imagine. We're there to love and appreciate them. They know that, and that makes all the difference.

JASON: We never witnessed physical violence against Christians in Niger, but in 2015 we came close. I took a team over in January, and while we were there, two French Muslim jihadists in Paris forced their way into the offices of a satirical newspaper that had published a cartoon image of the prophet Mohammad. The jihadists, who considered the cartoon to be blasphemy, killed twelve people and injured eleven others. Following the attack, millions of people worldwide demonstrated for peace, while smaller-scale attacks by other Muslims continued.

In January, days after our group left Niger to return home by way of Paris, Muslim protesters in Niamey set fire to Christian schools and churches—some that we had just visited. This was a tough time for me as the director of Schools for Niger, Africa. I was hurting for our partner schools halfway around the globe that had been affected by this evil act. Doubts creeped in as to whether or not it would be safe to ever take a team to Niger again. And how would I be able to recruit anyone for the next mission?

The most common question Haley and I get in meetings leading up to our mission trips is, "Is it safe?" Well, up until now I felt confident to say yes it was safe; we had not witnessed or experienced anything to say otherwise. But now one of the schools we had just been in seventy-two hours ago was burned down because it was Christian.

HALEY: I remember thinking this was going to scare previous travelers and keep them from returning with us to Niger. My heart was broken and aching for the Christians in Niger and more so for our dear friends. I cried and cried and asked my friend Cheryl to pray for me. As I was sharing the details with her, I picked up a brand-new Bible study book and randomly opened it. There on that page was a letter written to the person doing the study, which was me:

Dear _____,

You don't have to carry this grief or burden on your own. I welcome all those who are weary and heavy burden to come to me. On the days the grieve seems too much call on me [sic]. *Remember that I will never resist a broken or contrite heart (Psalm 51:17).*

Draw near to me and I will draw near to you. Remember that you do not serve one who cannot sympathize with your weakness. Allow the mourning to run its course. Some days you'll feel like you're taking steps forward other days you'll feel like you're taking steps backward. Some days you'll feel tired. Some days your energy will be renewed. So this process I'm going to reveal lesser priorities in your life and expand your ability to show compassion to others. Know that I am with you every step of the way. And I am the one who promises to wipe every tear from your eye (Revelation 21:4).

Your loving father.[7]

This was exactly what I needed to hear in that moment. God was so personal, and I felt that letter was Him speaking to me.

Three days later I went to Bible study, and a friend handed me a bag of items she had purchased for the people of Niger. Another reminder from above to keep walking in faith. I continued praying about my upcoming October team, praying, "Lord, if I am supposed to continue serving in Niger, then allow people to sign up for my team this week."

He answered those prayers, and I had three ladies sign up the same week! The Lord was faithful to confirm things for me time after time so that I would continue to walk in obedience to Him.

JASON: One of the realities of getting out of the boat is that now you are no longer confined to the comfort and small area of a floating vessel. Instead, you have this huge area of opportunity for ministry and love. We want to do more for the people of Niger than we're physically able to do in the short time that we're there, more to empower the people to build their own economic independence. We can't just give them stuff all the time. In the book *Toxic Charity*, Robert Lupton explains, "Giving to those in need what they could be gaining from their own initiative may well be the kindest way to destroy people. Our free food and clothing distribution encourages ever-growing handout lines, diminishing the dignity of the poor while increasing their dependency."[8]

We were very intentional to follow this line of thinking by supporting partner organizations in Niger and allowing them to decide what gets handed out and when. Lupton urges others to "promote entrepreneurship, invest in infrastructure, reinforce productive work, and to create producers, not beggars."[9] Feed a man a fish and he'll eat for a day; teach a man to fish and he'll eat for a lifetime. Volunteers often have different goals than those of the community and its leaders. We had to learn to listen to indigenous leadership and hear the dreams of the people, which were usually different from our own ideas of what we thought they needed.

Once during every mission trip, a half day is set aside for the people who live nearby to set up a market of sorts for the Americans to buy some of the mostly handmade crafts they have created. Some make things from textiles or iron, and others carve hippos and other animals from soapstone. Soapstone is a white stone the carvers take and file down into shapes and animals. They might color the stone with shoe polish or some other stain and then fire it. One of the soapstone carvers, Solomon, makes nativity scenes, a common purchase from any of the mission teams.

One day I was looking at Solomon's nativities, and I wondered what he knew about the pieces he had carved. Was he just creating something he knew the Christians from America would buy, or did he understand?

I held the soapstone infant in my hand and asked through an interpreter, "Do you know who this is?"

"That is Jesus," Solomon said.

"And do you know who Jesus is?" I asked.

"No," he said.

"You're carving Him every day," I said. "Would you like to know more about Him?"

"Okay," he said, a little skeptically.

For the next forty-five minutes, a translator, Phil Nichols, and I sat with Solomon and talked, preaching Jesus. We reached a point where he accepted Christ and allowed us to pray over him. Then we connected him with one of the missionaries so he could get plugged into a church, and then a missionary named Jeremy befriended Solomon and took him to Bible study and church regularly.

Solomon still carves nativities, but with a completely different point of view.

HALEY: The Christian pastors are doing a powerful work in this nation of Niger. Djibo is one of my favorite friends we have met during our time serving in Niger. He is a Christian preacher. One of the things that stands out to me about Djibo is his obedience to the Lord's calling on his life. When Djibo first moved outside the city into a village near the Niger River to begin his ministry work there, it took years of patience and preparation before he began to see the fruits of his labor. The small village where Djibo and his wife lived was more than 90 percent Muslim, like the rest of the country. A year after they moved, Djibo was still preaching to only his wife, yet he remained faithful.

Then there was a miraculous transformation. The community began embracing Djibo in an interesting way. The adults wouldn't come to his church; they were Muslim and said they were not going to change their beliefs. But they were willing to send their children to attend. He had almost all the children in the community and about ten adults.

As a team leader, I have the privilege of creating a schedule of the places we will visit and serve while in Niger. Jason had met Djibo on an earlier mission trip and said I should try to take our group by and see him. We were impressed by Djibo's commitment to the Lord, and I wanted the team to be a part of what the Lord had been doing out in this village and at Djibo's church. Djibo invited my team to host a vacation Bible school during the week for the children when we came back in October.

"You should prepare for more than a hundred kids," he said.

I couldn't imagine that more than one hundred kids would show up based on what I knew of his ministry in the past.

We packed plenty of Bible school supplies, and when we arrived, fifty children ranging from six months to six years old, wearing the most tattered clothing and some with no clothing at all, were standing inside the church's walled-in property. Djibo had built a handmade cinder block building, and inside it felt like a furnace in the afternoon sun, so we started outside.

As we began to interact with the children who were already there, our voices and their laughter radiated over the walls of this compound. Before we knew it, children began running through the rusted metal door in a constant flow over the next fifteen minutes. I looked at the team, I looked at Djibo, and as we counted all these barefoot children, the number totaled more than 150. It was obvious they hadn't had a bath in days or maybe weeks, and their clothes covered in dirt and stains desperately needed washing.

We placed mats on the hot, sandy ground for the children to sit, then we told Bible stories, which Djibo translated in their tribal language. We put on puppet shows, played games, and handed out candy and toys as our time that day ended. On Sunday morning, we made our way back to the church, and the building was packed so tight with kids and a few adults that I don't think we could have gotten another person in. A slight breeze blew through the windows, but it was really hot in there. Djibo had the children recite the Bible verses he and his wife had been teaching them week after week. My heart could have exploded! After all of these years the Lord had blessed the work that Djibo and his wife had been doing. This was worth the heat and sweating we endured for two hours that morning!

JASON: Leading teams became something I looked forward to each year. Haley and I knew we could go fast alone, but teams could go further together. The following January, I took my team back to see Djibo, and after he finished preaching to what seemed to be about eighty children, we as a team handed out cherry red "Jesus loves you" lollipops to each child. We said our goodbyes, and our translator from LINK began to lead us through a village that none of us had ever walked through before. The sights and smells were eye-opening to say the least. The crowd of children followed us and grabbed at our hands like we were pied pipers as we walked through probably the most impoverished village I had seen in Africa.

The kids were laughing, but the adults were not. They were just staring at these white Christian men walking through their village leading their children like we were some kind of celebrities. The stares reminded us that we were not celebrities. We were not even welcome.

Year after year, Haley would take her team back to teach children at Djibo's. In fact, all the LINK teams would visit his church and walk through this impoverished village. We smiled at the adults and tried to engage them, but with limited results.

Then the fundraising arm of Effective Ministries bought a grinder for the village so they could grind their millet. They presented it to the chief of the village in the name of Jesus, no strings attached. A gift. The chief was blown away by the generosity. They no longer had to grind the grain by hand. In fact, the grinder was so efficient, they could grind enough to sell and make a little money.

The chief told the missionaries that they and their pastors could visit the village any time.

Haley and I both continued to take our teams to the village. Then in January 2020, when I took my team, I saw in the middle of the village the most beautiful well I've ever seen in Niger. It had tile and faucets for running water in the middle of this poor, dusty village, like an oasis.

"It's beautiful," I said. "Who built it?"

"Muslims from Turkey," our guide said.

"Really? From Turkey?"

For decades this tired little group of people in faraway West Africa had lived in desperation until a few Christians from the other side of the world shared the love of Christ. Did our gift somehow draw the attention of Muslims more than two thousand miles away? Niger is more than 90 percent Muslim already. Did somebody in Turkey see us as a threat? They obviously see more than the grinder we gave a small village. They see the schools and orphanages we've built in the name of Christ.

The new well was not the only response to the inroads Christians are making in West Africa. Outside one of the orphanages we built, a shiny new mosque was constructed.

Literally right outside the door to the orphanage run by Christians. There's a new hospital and a university too. Christians didn't build them. They were all paid for by large groups from Muslim countries.

Yet even the Muslim leadership is under attack. Along Niger's southeastern border with Nigeria, eight hundred miles from Niamey, Islamist Boko Haram insurgents have terrorized Muslim civilian populations in their fight against the westernization of society.

Out of concern that insurgents will reach across the country, the US Embassy and the Nigerien government told us not to venture outside the city limits of Niamey.

These changes remind us that our time in Niger is limited. We believe the day will come when the Nigerien government prevents Christians from evangelizing openly. In the meantime, we will reach one soul at a time. We plant the seeds as long as we're allowed and let God take care of the rest.

"The harvest is plentiful but the workers are few. Ask the Lord of the harvest, therefore, to send out workers into his harvest field" (Matt. 9:37–38).

JASON AND HALEY: In leading teams to Niger we took this privilege very seriously and would pray and ask the Lord where we should go and what needs we could provide for the organizations we were serving. That could get expensive, and many people back in the US would ask what they could donate. We were so blessed by so many generous people over the years.

Over and over friends, family, travelers, and their friends and families would donate items—some that we had requested and some we had not. We always took everything, even things we hadn't requested, because we learned that if the Lord provided them, there was a need that we just didn't know about yet.

Over the years, the Lord's provision was another tool He used to increase our faith. Bedsheets, shoes, clothes, reusable diapers, school supplies, washcloths, soap, wall decals, pillowcases, food, funds for projects in country, and so on were all items the Lord provided every year! The Lord uses many believers to accomplish His purposes. Some of us physically went to serve, others donated items, others gave funds to cover projects, and still others prayed. In God's eyes, we all played an important role in reaching people for His kingdom.

Romans 12 teaches us as the body of Christ that we are all one body with different parts but working together to serve God and His kingdom on this earth. We are so thankful for the many generous believers who have donated resources to help reach the people of Niger for Christ all these years.

HALEY: We were planning our 2013 trip to Niger when Jason's cousin Cara called from Kentucky and said she was joining me for another mission. But something in her voice

Bilotti children's first mission to Niger, Africa

The board for Schools for Niger, Africa

Haley's first mission and picture with Rachid

Jason with Brielle at CSEN orphanage

Jason and Haley with Solomon, whom Jason led to Christ

Haley leading her first mission team, 2011

Children of Niger in a remote village

*Daily life in Niger—
carrying items
on their heads*

Cara's baptism in Niger River

Kristi with children on the medical team, 2009

Haley and Debbie on the medical team, 2009

A home in Niger

Haley playing ball with Joel at CSEN orphanage

Rachid visits Haley as she serves on the medical team in 2010

Playing Hot Potato with the children at CURE hospital

Children at Vacation Bible School

Jason with Momo, a Pittsburgh Steelers fan – at CSEN

Squatter homes in Niger

Houses in a Niger village

Niger transportation

Haley's team visits with ladies in prison

Village of Boubon

Rachid, Paulina, and Hunter at the sand dunes

Those eyes say so much!

Whitefield team at the school Paulina raised funds to build

*Women of Niger in a remote village, we
distributed reusable diapers to them*

Haley and Brielle

Another VBS

Local fishermen on the Niger River

Haley and Jason visit one of our SFNA schools during the pandemic

Haley holding a baby in an orphanage

Haley's team with Djibo and his family

Jason with a friend at CURE hospital

A widow holding her granddaughter

Haley and Jason at a CSEN orphanage

Women of Niger

Left to right: Kristi, Cheryl, Haley, and Luanne

was different. More emotional. I waited. "Haley," she said after a moment, "I want to be baptized."

My heart immediately leapt. "Cara, that's wonderful!" I said.

"In Niger," she said.

"Great!" I said.

"Niger changed my heart," she said.

I knew that. Niger changes the heart of everyone who goes there. But Cara had not grown up going to church. She hadn't understood the power of God, and she hadn't experienced the love of Jesus. Then, in a faraway land a world away from her home in Kentucky, she understood.

After Cara's first mission to Niger, she accepted Christ and wanted to share this publicly in the country where her "light bulb" moment took place.

"And I want to be baptized," she said, "in the Niger River."

Well, now that might be a little bit of a problem.

A beautiful river is a wonderful place to be baptized, just as Jesus was baptized in the Jordan. The cleansing water flows over you and you can feel the power of the Holy Spirit and the connection to our Savior. But the Niger River is one of the most polluted rivers in the world, with runoff from nearby towns and villages where indoor plumbing is almost nonexistent, not to mention hippos. I could only imagine the disease and parasites in the water as it flowed through the city.

I said a bit skeptically, "Okay," but I wasn't sure our LINK staff in Niger would go along.

I called to ask if Cara could be baptized in the river, and they, too, were concerned but open to the possibility. They had options for Cara: baptism in a pool at a missionary's home, in a tub inside a church, or in the river itself.

Cara insisted she wanted to be baptized in the river, so that was the plan.

A few weeks later we were in Niger, and during the church service they asked Cara and two other ladies who wanted to be baptized that day to come up for prayer. This moment was very moving for Cara as she felt the Holy Spirit's presence in a way in which she had never felt before. After we went to church on Sunday, we all headed to the river; kids were playing and women were washing clothes made with fabrics of every color the African culture has to offer.

Pastor Boureima and Pastor Boubacar rolled up their pant legs and stepped into the muddy brown colored water, and Edem was there to translate.

"When I was lifted up out of the water," she said, "I had this renewed sensation. I felt as if the old Cara was washed down the river just like the lily pads that floated by."

Cara's transformation of "new life in Christ" has been evident over the past several years. Cara will now pray out loud in a group of ladies. She loves to serve children in various forms, sharing the love of Jesus with them, and she has continued to serve on many missions trips with me. I am so thankful for her first "yes" and how the Lord has grown her faith through her servant heart.

SIX

CALLED TO ADOPT

JASON: In November 2009, I was back in Niger, visiting the orphanage where our sponsored child, Rachid, lived. After spending the day with him, I wrote this in my journal:

After lunch we rested for two hours before heading to the orphanage. This was the highlight. We took Christmas gifts for each child, and Santa delivered to each one. We helped them with a craft—a frame to send with a picture of themselves to their sponsors. We then watched fireworks with them. I held Rachid and Soumilla, while Souva, another child we sponsor, didn't let down her guard. I got very shook up while here, thinking about these kids without parents. We then returned to the Bible school for dinner, stew, and rice. I didn't eat much. God, what were you trying to tell me today at the orphanage?

On my next trip, I taught Rachid to thumb wrestle, and he didn't want to stop. We laughed and played together for hours; that was the most interaction I had ever had with him. Leaving Rachid and these children was more difficult this time for reasons that I didn't understand. After I came home from that trip, night after night I would wake up and feel the Lord saying to me, "Get him out." The vision was not scary or ghostlike. It was just the Lord showing me Rachid's face and speaking to me, "Get him out. Get him out. Get him out of that orphanage!"

This was not making sense to me. We had our boy and our girl, and we were done. That was exactly the family Haley and I had hoped for. So, I ignored the Lord's prompting for about three months. I didn't even mention it to Haley.

HALEY: During a mission in 2009, the children at the orphanage sang their songs, and then one of the ladies asked if any of the children could be adopted. I told her they could not, but I didn't know why. It was just under-stood. I said I would contact Michael Thaler when we returned to the States and find out why. When I asked Michael, he didn't know much more than I did, but he said he would learn more.

Three months later, Michael and his wife, Sharon, came to Atlanta and we met for dinner.

JASON: I still had not told Haley about the Lord's prompting me to get Rachid out of the orphanage, and she had not told me she was going to bring up the adoption issue with Michael. When she asked if it was true the children could not be adopted, Michael said, "Actually, you can, but it's very difficult. Sharon and I have decided to begin the process ourselves."

And I'm thinking, *Oh, no, no, no.*

Then they told us about two laws in Niger that made it difficult for Americans to adopt there: children older than five could not be adopted, and couples who had biological children could not adopt Nigerien children. They could not find any records going back at least fourteen years of any American family adopting a child from Niger.

I was sad thinking of all the children in the village who literally stared through the orphanage gate because they'd rather be inside than out on the street, where many were walking around in diapers or naked, hungry, and dirty.

As I listened, I knew it was time to tell Haley what God had been saying to me about Rachid. Somehow, despite the roadblocks Michael and Sharon described, God had a different plan for this child.

HALEY: I came home one afternoon, and Jason was sitting in the keeping room of our home. "I need to talk to you," he said, and the tone of his voice was not good. I sat down, and he began to cry. His tears triggered my own tears. Jason is not one to cry easily or often, so my heart sank. What is wrong? Is he sick?

He began to share how the Lord had been waking him up at night with visions of Rachid's face and telling him to "get him out!" The dream had come back to him on several nights. Jason had prayed about the dreams and was certain that God was calling us to adopt Rachid. You see, the Lord knew He had to give this vision to Jason, because if I had been given the vision and had brought it to Jason, he might not have agreed to adopting Rachid. I cried as I listened to my husband share what he had experienced, knowing only God could move his heart in this way. I told Jason that I was in full support of exploring the possibility of adopting Rachid.

We knew it would not be easy, but we knew this was what the Lord was calling us to. During that time period, Jason and I would play Lincoln Brewster's recording of "Everlasting God," written by Brenton Brown and Ken Riley. The song tells us that our strength rises up when we wait on

God. The lyrics call Him a "Strong Deliverer" and tell us that, because of the hope we have in Him, we won't faint or even grow weary! We would play it over and over, and this gave us the strength to keep walking by faith and see the adoption through:

> You are the everlasting God
> The everlasting God
> You do not faint
> You won't grow weary
> You're the defender of the weak
> You comfort those in need
> You lift us up on wings like eagles[10]

PAULINA: I vividly remember the four of us sitting at the kitchen table, and Hunter was all in on the idea of adopting Rachid. He immediately said, "Yes." To be honest, I was very cautious. I liked my family. I liked having my big brother. I liked my two parents, and—remember, I was also really young—I thought, *I don't want to be outnumbered by another boy.* I just wanted it to be us. The four of us. Then my parents said, "Okay, well, why don't you pray about it?" So, I grudgingly, angrily started praying about it, and the Lord began to soften my heart. The next morning, I came down for breakfast and told my parents that I wanted them to adopt Rachid. "Yeah, let's do this. I think I do want another brother. I want Rachid to come over."

HUNTER: What convinced me was thinking about where Rachid was coming from and the opportunity we could give him. It goes back to "the first shall be last and the last shall be first." And it's about blessing others and giving others an opportunity. Because my parents were able and willing to do that, I felt the same way. And I thought bringing somebody else into our home would be a huge blessing and opportunity for us as well.

HALEY: We contacted Bethany Christian Services, an organization that supports vulnerable children, refugees, and families around the world, for help adopting Rachid. That's when we began to experience the complexity of the journey we were embarking on, beginning with the Hague Convention. The Hague Convention on the Protection of Children and Co-operation in Respect of Intercountry Adoption was a new agreement among most of the world's countries to regulate adoptions for the best interests of the children. The United States was part of the Hague Convention, but Niger was not. That meant that Bethany Christian Services could not help us in Niger, and they were limited in how much they could do for us in the US. We would have to hire someone to do everything for us in Niger, and if we were successful there, another agency would have to help us at home, conducting background checks on Jason and me that would be required for us to adopt a child.

Despite the obvious hurdles, Dave Johansson a missionary in Niger, connected us with a lawyer there who said, "Yes, yes, we can have this done in three months."

Three months! We had things to do to get ready!

Rachid also needed to prepare for a life in the United States. Dave and his wife, Hope, agreed to move Rachid from the orphanage into their home, where they could teach him how to bathe and brush his teeth and other basic hygiene skills. Dave and Hope had three boys of their own, and they found an English tutor who could work with Rachid a few times a week. We felt like we were off and running. We could see the Lord's hand already working on our behalf.

JASON: Some of our friends thought we were crazy to do this. How could it possibly work? Different race, different nationality, different culture. There was so much that had to come together for this to work.

Haley and I wanted support from our own families, and we didn't know what kind of reaction to expect. But when we told them what we were planning, they all said, "This is amazing. Let's do it!"

Yet, even as we grew more excited every day, and as we prepared our children and our parents and our friends for this tremendous change in all of our lives, we wondered if we should even be trying. The laws of Niger were against us, despite the encouragement we received from our lawyer there.

My fourth mission to Niger was in November 2010, and we had twelve travelers from Richmond, Virginia, and eleven travelers from Atlanta, Georgia. During this mission, Dave Johansson a missionary, took me to see the notary, also a lawyer, about adopting Rachid. She was a very serious lady, almost scary to be in the presence of, but we left there with a document that said Rachid was now Rachid Bilotti. I cried in the truck with Dave and thanked him for all the work he had done to get us this far. I called Haley and we cried together, as I could barely get the story and words out of my mouth. As I rejoined the team, I will never forget Phil being so encouraging to me. I wrote in my journal, "Cool to be obedient! Rachid my third child, my new son!"

The lawyer, Mazet, continued to say he would have it all wrapped up in a bow for us in three months. Then three months became eight months, and just before the hearing before the judge, world events changed the course of Rachid's life. On May 2, 2011, nearly four thousand miles from Niger, US Navy SEALs killed al-Qaeda leader Osama bin Laden in Pakistan. Two days later, our lawyer stood before a Muslim judge in Niger and presented his case for Rachid to be adopted by a Christian family in the United States.

The judge was clearly affected by bin Laden's death and said he would not allow a child to leave Niger to go West and live with a Christian family. His stated objection was that our "foundational reasoning for adopting Rachid was not strong." Then he told Mazet to get out of his courtroom!

Dave called with the ruling, and the crushing answer made no sense to us. I had heard so clearly from the Lord to do this. What had I misunderstood? Dave said we could appeal the ruling to a three-judge panel, and Mazet encouraged us to do that. So we did, but there were more delays.

Maybe we shouldn't have been surprised by the pace of the process. In the year Rachid was born, according to the United Nations, there were only eight intercountry adoptions in all of Niger. Eight children adopted to families outside of Niger. We thought of intercountry adoptions as a regular thing here, with thousands of children coming to the United States every year. But not from Niger, and the system there seemed unable or unwilling to handle our petition.

While we waited, Haley and I continued to travel to Niger regularly, and we visited with Rachid, now eleven years old, every time. It was important to know that Rachid wanted to come home with us, yet we didn't want to get his hopes up only to be disappointed. I sat with him and explained what we were trying to do, as best I could, and I asked, "Do you want to come and live in America?"

He gave me a resounding yes. That said, I knew his only ideas of America had come from Marvel movies he had watched on DVDs in the orphanage.

As we were praying for Rachid and our friends in Niger every day, we were expanding our scope in the US to generate much-needed resources for Schools for Niger, Africa (or SFNA). I chaired the board of directors for SFNA, and Howe Rice was our vice chair. Howe remained incredibly focused on building less expensive schools to create more opportunities for kids to continue their education beyond elementary school, and I wanted to build model schools—more expensive but higher quality to inspire students and communities. That tension was healthy for the board, and it pushed us to do our best work. It wasn't an "either-or," but a "both-and."

God asks us to do our work with excellence, and we all agreed that providing an exemplary Christian education for potential future leaders of Niger would have a profound effect on the nation. Our responsibility, then, was to build Christ-centered schools to teach the gospel of Jesus Christ and offer academic excellence.

We committed to building quality classrooms, and we would consider additional facilities as requested. We would help raise funds for scholarships and to increase pay for teachers. One of the most difficult tasks, we found, was staffing schools with well-trained Christian teachers. In a country where 94 percent of the population is Muslim, finding a Christian teacher was nearly impossible. Also, to be a teacher in Niger, you could teach below whatever level you had passed. In other words, a middle school graduate could teach elementary school, so as you can imagine, the quality of education being taught wasn't that strong.

We also committed to quality leadership from our board and a biblical approach to fundraising, and to that end I participated in a training program by Ministry Ventures led by Boyd Bailey. This was a yearlong training program for nonprofits, for which I received a certification.

To generate more funds and raise interest further in the US, Don Whitney, whom I had met two years earlier at our first dodgeball tournament, had suggested we work together to create the World Games, adding three-on-three soccer, cornhole, and moonwalks for the younger children. We could attract hundreds of teams and thousands of participants.

Kennesaw State University had agreed to host the World Games on their athletic field, with Chick-fil-A and Walmart agreeing to be lead sponsors. We were meeting with the KSU president and athletic director and others working out the details, when Dave's number popped up on my phone, from over in Niger.

My heart raced as I stepped out into the hall to talk, expecting news about Rachid; Dave said the judges had denied our appeal. It was over, and my tears began to flow in my disappointment over losing the possibility of adopting Rachid. How could I have been so wrong? I paced in the hallway for a few minutes, wiping my eyes and regaining my composure, then went back into the room and finished the meeting.

Afterward Don and I were driving back, and I was trying to explain it to him, but he didn't understand. "There are so many kids from China being adopted," he said. "You and Haley could adopt a child from there."

We must have heard that suggestion ten or fifteen times from people who knew us and loved us but didn't understand that God had made it very clear to us that it was *Rachid*. God didn't say, "Adopt a *kid*." He said, "Get *Rachid* out."

That night Haley and I prayed together and reconfirmed that we were in agreement in our understanding of God's will. A few days later I was telling Lawson Bailey about our latest disappointment, and he reminded me, "God told you to get Rachid out. Maybe God never meant for you to have him. Maybe it's just about finding him a place to live."

It was a possibility I had not considered. Lawson might be right. It stinks if he is, and if I misread God's message to me, but he might be right.

Dave and Hope were headed home for a much-needed furlough and would be gone for six months. We prayed about what to do next and connected with a Nigerien Christian pastor, Bouremia, and asked if he could take Rachid into his home. He had a boy the same age as Rachid. Bouremia said, "I'll take him in. It is what we do."

Those powerful words ring clearly in my heart today: "It is what we do." Again, someone was willing to step out of the boat and not just sit there. What a great testament of putting others ahead of self.

Bouremia asked if we could offer financial support for Rachid's schooling, and we did, through the LINK organization. We also sent over money to purchase a motorcycle for a LINK employee, Aime, who could give Rachid a ride to school each day. I must admit I never imagined I would be praying for God to keep one of our children safe each day on the back of a motorcycle! But this was our reality; we officially had a second son in Niger, who we couldn't bring home. In the meantime, Michael and Sharon had been unable to adopt a particular little girl from Niger, and they began the process with another child, so we were no longer on parallel tracks with them.

Then Bethany Christian Services called out of the blue and said they would like to do more to help us. Haley explained that the process in Niger had ended. Rachid was staying there. However, we decided to complete our part of the process with Bethany just in case the status changed. By this time, we had spent thousands of dollars on an adoption process that was dead in the water across the Atlantic.

We met a lawyer in Atlanta who suggested we use a process called a "simple adoption," because Rachid's case was complicated: his mother was still living. She was in difficult circumstances: addicted and forced to sell her body to make enough money to barely survive, so she had abandoned her children to the orphanage. We were skeptical. There was an implication that we would have to come back to Niger to formalize everything after a period of time. What if Rachid's mom changed her mind? We didn't want to bring him here only for him to have to go back. That would be crushing for our family and for him. But he insisted that he had completed multiple simple adoptions, and if we could bring Rachid into our home, he could manage the legal aspects and we wouldn't have to worry. After more prayer, we decided to go with it. Yes, the process seemed "dead in the water," but once again we trusted the Lord and stepped out onto that water.

In December 2011, we were introduced to a lady in Niger named Ester, who introduced us to another lawyer there, Madame Lopy, to handle our case. Madame Lopy had been a judge previously, and she knew the judges working on our case. She was also a Christian. She convinced us that she could plead our case successfully, but she needed Rachid's birth certificate.

We wondered if this would even be possible. Rachid's mother lived in a small, impoverished hut. She didn't own a bed, much less a filing cabinet or safe to keep important paperwork in. Apparently, though, she had learned the importance of keeping her children's birth certificates, because when someone from the orphanage went out and asked, she had it in a box. That's when we learned that Rachid was born in 1998. He was thirteen, a year older than we thought.

Missionary Beki Rohan, now Helwig, was a huge help and support for us during this time. She was able to take Rachid to get his required shots and physical to be able to leave the country. She also was able to help us with different forms of paperwork, getting them to the proper places. We all thought Beki was a rock star for Jesus! Here was a young lady, who rode a motorcycle everywhere, living alone in a remote village outside of Niamey. Living with no running water, no technology, no electricity. Simply living by faith and trusting the Lord to protect and provide for her day by day. This was convicting for both Haley and me. Beki was not sitting, she was willing to sink, and I visualize that motorcycle of hers being a jet ski flying across the water, or sand, for Jesus.

Madame Lopy did not promise miracles, and we knew the process would take time. Each time we visited Niger, we tried to help Rachid understand the process so he would be patient. We learned that he was the patient one. He's the most resilient person I've ever known. Haley or I would explain the latest delay, and he would be sad in the moment, but he would say, "Okay." We would be torn up emotionally, and he would be fine.

In my final journal entry for my January 2012 trip, I wrote,

> Went to airport. Hard to say goodbye to Rachid! We both cried. He stood up top and watched us leave thru a cage/fence. I have to get him out of there!! Please God!!

We finally got the call in early November 2012 that we could come to Niger and bring Rachid home. Everything was approved. Three years had lapsed since we first got the call from God to adopt Rachid, and he had grown from a small nine-year-old boy to a teen of fourteen. My brother, Chad, sent Haley and me a letter that summed up our years of pursuing Rachid by his name, R-A-C-H-I-D.

You two were **Relentless** and **Attacking** after God put this on your heart to make this happen.

It takes **Courage** to follow God's plan when it is something you never thought you would do.

God is **Honored** by your trust in Him. You two **Ignored** the doubters, friends, and family who thought this was crazy and could not happen. You ignored the lawyers telling you this could not happen. You ignored the Muslim judge who said it could not happen. You ignored Satan, stayed the course, and trusted God's plan.

The **Determination** you demonstrated in not giving up the pursuit was incredible.

I could not be more proud to be "Uncle Chad" to Rachid.

We left Atlanta on Thanksgiving Day, and when we arrived in Niger, we were fingerprinted and questioned even more. Rachid had to get his passport approved by the US embassy, and ironically, that's where we ran into bumps in the road. An American in the embassy delayed his approval day after day. It was as if he was trying to prove his authority.

At first, his concerns seemed legitimate. He wanted to ensure that we had been vetted and approved appropriately by Nigerien authorities to adopt Rachid. Then he asked us to bring Rachid's mother to the embassy. She had already been questioned and had assured the Nigerien judge that having Rachid live with us was her desire, but the embassy official wanted to see it for himself.

Another delay felt like another opportunity for everything to fall apart. We left the embassy discouraged that we still were not finished. Later that day, when it was time to return, Dave went to the hut and asked Rachid's mom to come with him to the embassy. About the same time, Haley, Rachid, and I were walking back to the embassy for the final time, we hoped, and I saw Rachid's mom walking the same direction. She was pregnant and had another small child wrapped up on her back. She looked tired and in pain, as if she were sick. When she turned toward us, there was no expression on her face. No acknowledgment of Rachid. "Haley, you and Rachid go that way," I said quickly. I didn't know how it would go if Rachid saw his mom and she said nothing.

HALEY: It was too late. Their eyes met, then she turned back and looked straight ahead again. She didn't speak or even nod. For me, a mother, that was a crushing moment for me, one of the most heartbreaking moments I can imagine. We wanted her to allow us to bring her son home with us, yet we wanted with all our hearts for her to express her love for Rachid the last time she would see him. My heart broke for Rachid over the feeling of rejection he must experience with the loss of his biological mother. Her heart seemed like it was made of stone. My mind was racing with so many thoughts and questions that I would never have the answers to. I began to pray for Rachid and his mother that God would do what only He could do in their hearts in this moment. I decided that with every chance we had, we would show Rachid that he was loved and special to us.

JASON: I went to the embassy gate alone, and the guard there hassled me about coming back and forth. Maybe she thought I was a security risk. But she let me in, and Rachid's mother came in too. They led us to a room where we waited, just the two of us plus the baby swaddled on her back, unable to communicate for more than an hour.

I prayed and asked God for peace to help us cross this last hurdle, but I couldn't stop thinking about what could go wrong. What if she changed her mind? What if she doesn't understand? She smelled so bad from body odor and possibly urine from the baby, and I felt compassion for her. If all went well, we would be taking Rachid out of this world to a place with fresh running water and clean showers, a soft bed and three healthy meals every day. His mother would remain here in her poverty, living in a tiny hut, selling herself to buy enough food to survive another day. We needed to help her, too, but we could not before we had final approval for Rachid to leave. We could not risk the appearance of bribery.

They finally took us to another room where the embassy official began to interview Rachid's mom. She said she understood the process and that Rachid would be leaving for the United States with us. He asked if we had paid her any money, and she said we had not. Then he asked if she had given her permission for us to become Rachid's adoptive parents, and she said yes.

Finally. I exhaled and felt myself relaxing. But the official did not say "okay" or "very good" or anything indicating we were good to go. He said he would let us know shortly.

I turned to Rachid's mother and thanked her, then I went out and found Haley and Rachid. We felt better than ever that we could go home soon, but we weren't there yet. It would be another day before the embassy notified us that Rachid was free to go home with us. We went back to the US embassy one last time, ready to beg the man to approve Rachid coming home with us. Finally, for reasons I still do not understand, he simply said, "Okay," and we were on our way. Nothing had changed in a week. Why did the American embassy make us wait?

Even after all that, there was still the prospect of having to bring Rachid back. We were still not completely clear about the simple adoption process. "Fear not!" God tells us, but it's so hard to shut the fear away. You may feel unmovable obstacles facing you; if so, stand still with courage and watch God part the waters for you to walk ahead of Him.

RACHID: I remember being excited about being on a plane for the first time. I watched movies during the first few hours and eventually fell asleep during the last few hours of the long flight. I sat with my new dad during the flights. We played FIFA soccer in the Paris airport on some TV-type game podium. After we made it through customs, I can still recall seeing lots of people standing there with signs welcoming me to this country and family. This was overwhelming for me while also exciting and confusing; all of this was new to me.

HALEY: From that moment forward, the days became a wide-eyed blur for Rachid. Airports and airplanes crossing the Mediterranean Sea and then the Atlantic Ocean. We landed in Atlanta and stood in the customs line. They led us to a different area than we normally reentered the United States, and we stood in line for what seemed like a long time. When we got to the front, we showed the official the papers we had for Rachid, and he handed him his passport. The man had a big stamp that he used to hit the papers—*stamp, stamp, stamp*—and Rachid's passport. "Welcome," he said. "Here is your green card. You are welcome to stay."

"Wait," Jason said. "What did you say? What does that mean?"

The man pointed to the papers he had handed back to us and said, "He's officially part of your family now."

Well, we could have floated out of the airport. It was like the weight of the entire world was lifted. After three years of prayers and tears, thousands of dollars sent, two no's, the death of a judge, additional funds sent, two lawyers, and boundless love, a Nigerien judge and the US State Department, guided by God's hand, had given us a son, and this customs officer had made the announcement to us. Rachid was officially part of our family. This was not a "simple adoption." Bethany Christian Services later verified that we had full custody of Rachid.

We hurried through baggage claim and up to the terminal, where friends met us with signs and hugs and more tears. Hunter and Paulina, meeting Rachid for the first time, hugged him immediately and held him for a long time. I wondered what must be going through Rachid's mind and heart. All of these people hugging him. This would have been the most affection Rachid had been given his whole life. It was ten o'clock for those of us still on Nigerien time, but it was just approaching dinnertime in Atlanta, so we drove to our Vinings restaurant, where his first meal in his new home country was Chick-fil-A. We drove home and showed him his bedroom. We were all exhausted, so we didn't stay up late to talk. In the beginning of our adoption process, when things were looking really good with our early appeal in Niger, we prepared Rachid's bedroom for his arrival home. Friends had advised us against it, but we thought we were so close!

Then Rachid didn't come.

As the process dragged on and we longed for our son to be home, we walked past that bedroom every time we went downstairs or back up again. The room was so empty and so quiet.

About the same time, Jason read the book *The Circle Maker* by Mark Batterson, which suggests "drawing prayer circles around your dreams" in your mind or in reality.[11] From that day forward, every morning Jason circled Rachid's empty bed and prayed, *Jesus, if it is Your will, bring Rachid to this bed.* Over and over, he prayed those words. Someone with less faith might have seen Jason's circle prayers day after day as pointless. I believed. I knew God had made this calling clear to us and would make a way in His time.

And now God had answered our prayers. Rachid was home, sleeping in his bed. Three months turned into three long years, yet God was working. Rachid was being taught English, and Hunter and Paulina's prayer life grew as they were pleading with the Lord for the adoption to be approved. Our marriage grew stronger as we prayed for miracles and watched as the Lord worked on our behalf. Isaiah 64:4 says, "Since ancient times no one has heard, no ear has perceived, no eye has seen any God besides you, who acts on behalf of those who wait for him."

Another song we relied on during this whole process, but especially in the final months, was "Never Once" by Matt Redman, Jason Ingram, and Tim Wanstall:

> Scars and struggles on the way
> But with joy our hearts can say
> Yes, our hearts can say

Never once did we ever walk alone
Never once did You leave us on our own
You are faithful, God, You are faithful[12]

SEVEN

CALLED TO ENDURANCE

PAULINA: I remember the first day Rachid came home like it was yesterday. Riding in our family friends' hot van after school to get to the airport and meet our parents and our new brother sparked lots of anxious excitement. Hunter and I were both so eager to meet Rachid, we sprinted out of the van as soon as it was in park and ran inside the busiest airport in the world. Scanning through the different faces, we waited with signs that welcomed our new family member to his new home in Atlanta.

Finally catching a wave from the escalator, Hunter and I sprinted over and embraced our parents as though they had been gone for years. Realizing we were being rude, I turned around to meet my brother. He looked scared and over-whelmed with his little chipped-tooth smile that peeped through, and we hugged for the first time. When we got home, we wanted to show him the house and the basement—just show him everything! My parents, being concerned that he was overwhelmed, cautioned us to take it slow. We asked Rachid what he thought, but he didn't say much. He smiled, but he wouldn't say a word. I was thinking, *Is it going to be like this forever? Is he ever going to talk to us?*

Then a little later, Hunter, Rachid, and my dad went outside and started playing basketball, and I could see them communicating those little interactions while they played. They were laughing and talking, and they understood each other.

Later we were teaching him English words, and it was really frustrating for him sometimes. He pronounced *earth* as "earf." Hunter tried to teach him the "th" sound, but, again, it was frustrating for him trying to learn a different language. For the first year, he was still trying to learn English, so he seemed like a shy guy, but let me tell you, my brother is the opposite of shy.

JASON: A few days after Rachid came home with us, we had a party to celebrate with friends who had been praying for him and for us for years. All the boys went outside to play soccer and, of course, Rachid joined them. And he played barefoot. I told him, as best I could given the language issues, that wasn't going to work. But he insisted, even in December in Atlanta. He had never worn shoes to play soccer.

Boys in Niger play soccer all the time, always barefoot and usually in the dusty street with two rocks at each end for goals. Whenever I took a mission team over, we played with them. Rachid was as good as any of his friends, but he didn't stand out.

Then when Haley and I went to bring Rachid home, Dave and Hope had a goodbye party for him, and he invited all his friends. The adults were still eating when the kids got up and went outside to play. I walked outside to watch, and Rachid was absolutely taking over the game with his skill set, juking guys and dribbling right past them to score. I started feeling giddy, like, "Oh my gosh, we've got a soccer player on our hands!"

Soccer was always my sport. Our team south of Atlanta won two youth soccer state championships, and I attended a two-year college in north Georgia on a soccer scholarship. I mention this so you'll understand that I've seen some really good soccer players, and Rachid, with his pure, raw talent, was potentially a really good soccer player. But first, we had to get him into school.

HALEY: There was no way we could get Rachid into a traditional school when he arrived in December. He was fourteen years old, but he was on a sixth- or seventh-grade level. And, of course, he did not speak English. Our goal was to prepare him to attend Whitefield Academy with Hunter and Paulina. I homeschooled him from December until springtime and realized it was more than I could handle alone. We found a tutor who had previously been at Whitefield, and she worked with Rachid on all of his subjects. (Looking back, it might have been better to focus on teaching Rachid English first, then everything else might have come more easily.) Whitefield let us rent one of their modules, and that allowed us to take all three of the kids to school together. At the end of the school year, though, Whitefield told us that Rachid was probably not going to get in there. The challenge for them was that Rachid had no academic history, no official scores for them to evaluate.

JASON: Rachid hadn't been with us long before we saw that school and language would not be his only challenges; racism would also come into play. We were sponsoring a golf tournament south of Atlanta to raise money for SFNA. Rachid was not in school yet—he was with a tutor every day—so he had flexibility in his schedule to go with Haley and me to the tournament and see how people in the United States were helping kids he knew.

We arrived early to set up, and then I took him over to the pro shop to look around. We split up, both looking at clothes and equipment, when I noticed a guy behind the counter staring at Rachid, just watching and watching. He tapped another guy and nodded toward Rachid, and the other guy started watching him too.

I could feel anger building inside of me. These men thought Rachid was going to steal something.

"Hey, guys," I said strongly, "that's my son. We're good."

"Oh, no, no, no," the guy behind the counter sheepishly exclaimed. "We know that."

It was the first time in my life I had ever experienced racism, and it was because I had a Black child. This was going to be an issue Rachid would face for the rest of his life.

Not too long after that, Rachid and I were in a restaurant, and he was a few steps behind me. A customer asked if he could refill her water. I stopped and said, politely, "He's my son."

"Oh, I didn't mean anything," she said defensively, which made it worse.

"It's fine," I said in a way that let her know that it wasn't, and we walked on.

HALEY: Rachid continued his tutoring through the summer, and we prayed that Whitefield might change their decision, but they made it clear it was not going to work.

Jason and I didn't believe continued one-on-one tutoring was the answer either. Rachid loved sports, especially soccer, and he needed that outlet. He also needed to be with other kids his age. After school, he and Hunter spent a lot of time together. We began praying that the Lord would open a door for Rachid somewhere until he was prepared well enough academically to attend Whitefield.

HUNTER: As soon as Rachid got here, I considered him family. What was mine was his. My parents were his parents, and my sister was his sister now. I really didn't hold anything back from day one. And I think that had to do with my parents and how they raised us. I never really felt like reserving or holding anything back.

Mornings were tough at first. Rachid and I shared a bathroom with only one sink, and that was a challenge when we were trying to get ready at the same time. I hadn't prepared myself for that kind of change—how close we would be living and how much space I was used to.

After school most days, Rachid and I went to my friend's house next door, and we played soccer or basketball constantly. Rachid was very athletic and always wanted to play with us. He didn't go to our school, so my friends didn't see him there, but he connected with them and made friends in our neighborhood games.

At first, I was a little jealous of how good Rachid could dribble the ball. I was envious of his technical skill. But I realized I had certain skills and things that he didn't have. We played different positions—he played attack and forward up top, and I was on the defensive side, so we thought differently and saw things differently. He was trying to score, and I was trying to prevent people from scoring. We would practice out in the yard, and he would be trying to score, and I'd be trying to defend, and we'd be helping each other out in those ways.

He always hung close to me, and even though he understood more and more of the words we were saying, he would look to me for a nod or some signal. Then after a few months, he came out of his shell and was talking with everybody, even if we had to figure out the words.

RACHID: To this day, whenever we go somewhere as a family, people usually don't think I am with the other four white people, which is now my family. Sometimes it bothers me and sometimes it doesn't. I can tell people don't do it on purpose; I just wish they wouldn't assume.

HALEY: When Rachid arrived in the US, he could understand more English than he could communicate back to us. We had to be so patient with him as he learned the language and how to live in a culture that was so different from the one he had known all his life. Rachid would be in the shower for at least thirty minutes enjoying this luxury, because his upbringing included bathing outside while standing in a bucket with water dumped over his head. The children are clean for a matter of minutes, then they step out of the "shower" bucket and their feet immediately become dusty and covered with sand as they walk back to their rooms to sleep for the night.

Rachid has shared with us that many nights the children would sleep outside because it was cooler outside than inside.

He also had to learn that he didn't have to stash snacks and that, if he was hungry, there was plenty of food. I once walked into his room to put away laundry, and there was a lamp that had smoke coming off the top of it. Rachid had taken a bag of chips and had hidden it on top of the light bulb. When the light was turned on, the bag of chips began melting over the light bulb and had almost caught fire. I quickly began to realize how different American life truly would be for Rachid and how we would need to explain many differences of our culture to him.

Rachid was learning to ride his bike in the first few weeks he had arrived in America. He was riding down our steep hill to the bottom of the cul-de-sac with no hands, and he hit the curb and ran into our mailbox. Thankfully, he did not break any bones, but then he was scared to tell us that he had torn up his bike and our mailbox.

Hunter encouraged him to come tell Mom and Dad, but Rachid was too afraid, so Hunter had to inform us of the news. We showed Rachid that grace and love exist in a family.

Haley and I began to teach him that trust was the key and foundation to every relationship.

The first time I took Rachid to Costco, I had never seen a child's eyes so big in my entire life. He could not understand the concept of free food (samples) that Costco was handing out. A child who had only one meal a day at times, maybe two, was allowed to go into a store and eat unlimited free samples.

There was also a time when I saw Rachid in his and Hunter's bathroom with the door open holding a small razor blade in his hand. He was trying to trim his nails. I asked him where he found the razor blade, and he walked over and picked up the handheld pencil sharpener he had gotten the blade out of. Rachid had never used fingernail clippers before and had no idea what they were. I was able to show him the proper tool to cut our fingernails. I could only imagine in Rachid's mind how we as Americans really do have so much. At the end of a few weeks, I realized how much Rachid was having to adapt to American culture and our way of life that was completely opposite of how he had grown up.

JASON: We still didn't have the school situation figured out, and one day I drove over to Cumberland Christian Academy. I hadn't told Haley that I was going; I just was looking. It was summer, and I didn't see anybody around, so I walked over to the chapel on campus. The door was unlocked, and when

I stepped inside an older man invited me to come on in. I sat down and immediately broke down crying. The man must have wondered what was happening, this stranger walking in and weeping. He was very kind.

He introduced himself then said, "Tell me what's wrong."

I shared the whole story, our dream of having all of our children at Whitefield, not two different schools, that I was chair of the board there, how we wanted the best for Rachid, this boy we had brought to the United States, and how we didn't know where to turn.

He told me a bit about himself, and I realized that I had been at Berry College with his son. The more we talked, the more I began to believe that I was right where God wanted me to be at this moment. He had brought me to this place for more than comfort.

"We're here to help," he said, and he put me in touch with the school administration.

At home that night, I told Haley about Cumberland Christian, and we prayed our thanks and asked for wisdom and direction. Over the next few days, we met with the school administration, and we all realized this could work for Rachid.

The logistics wouldn't be easy. Cumberland Christian was in the opposite direction from Whitefield, so getting Rachid there in the morning and home in the afternoon was a challenge. And Rachid had so much to learn. We needed help. Haley spoke with my cousin Cara, who lived in Kentucky, while on their last mission in Niger. Cara loved to serve others and had a great skill set to be my assistant, managing payroll, insurance, and other financial needs in the restaurant, and she loved Rachid. She agreed and quickly became much more than my assistant at work. She was like a "team mom," cheerleader, peacemaker, birthday and anniversary celebrator, and a listening ear to team members.

I drove Rachid to school in the mornings, and that gave us time to work on his vocabulary skills and also just spend time together. Cara picked him up in the afternoons, and Haley picked up Hunter and Paulina.

HALEY: There were so many cultural issues that Rachid didn't understand about us and we didn't understand about him. From the moment they could talk, we had taught Hunter and Paulina to be thankful. We taught them to apologize when they hurt somebody. Rachid was not familiar with any of that. He was a teenager who had never been taught to show his appreciation. When he made a mistake or disobeyed, he did not apologize. And, frankly, that was discouraging for all of us.

Our children also knew they could trust us, and we knew we could trust them. Rachid did not understand that. He didn't know who he could trust.

JASON: The orphanage had been a tough place for Rachid to grow up as a little kid. When he came to our house, he must have wondered if we would be any different. Would he have to lie or steal or cheat to get by? Would we reach for the switch if he did something wrong?

Early on, when he messed up and we asked him about it, his instinct was to lie to avoid what he thought would be the consequences. He always seemed to anticipate major consequences for any mistake. We needed to show him that he could trust us, but that would take time.

That was just one of the issues we were trying to understand when we sought help from a family counselor. The counselor gave us a piece of advice that I've shared dozens of times to other dads: stop asking questions if you already know the answer. If you see a child take a cookie from the cookie jar, don't ask, "Did you take another cookie?" You may think they will take responsibility for their action, but too often they will not, and then what? Now you have a lie on top of the disobedience. And if you punish them for the lie, then they must wonder why you asked the question in the first place if you already knew the answer.

The counselor told us to avoid all that and focus on the disobedience. Say instead, "We told you not to take another cookie. Why did you do that?"

HALEY: The hardest times seemed to always happen when Jason was in Niger for a week or ten days. One day, something happened at school, and Rachid lied about it. I was so upset I didn't know what to do. So I went to his room to talk, and I got real serious with him. "Rachid, you claim to be a Christian," I said, "but if you're truly a Christian and the Holy Spirit is living inside of you, then when you sin, there should be some conviction going on there, right? That's the Holy Spirit's job, to convict us when we do wrong if we're truly His child."

We sat on his bed for a long time talking, and I was asking some hard questions, which led Rachid to tell me that he had never truly asked Jesus to come into his heart.

I spoke quietly and said, "I can help you through that if you want me to, but it has to be your decision. You can't be doing this to please me. It has to be for yourself."

We ended the conversation there to give Rachid time to think about his decision. He came to me later, and he was crying. We prayed together, and he accepted Christ.

I could immediately see the change in his heart, but like every Christian, Rachid still struggled. All do. Even the apostle Paul struggled with sin: "I have the desire to do what is good, but I cannot carry it out. For I do not do the good I want to do, but the evil I do not want to do—this I keep on doing" (Rom. 7:18–19).

It would take a long time for Rachid to understand the grace and forgiveness of Jesus, but we were on that road to understanding together. Rather than me being frustrated with him, I had more compassion as I tried to help him connect dots and overcome the weakness that led to the lying. This was a battle for him. Satan preys on our weaknesses, and Rachid would have another small issue a couple of months later. The first time or two when that happened, he would revert to the lying, and I would remind him that was not who he was anymore. It was so much easier for me to have compassion, knowing that I was trying to truly help him get on the right track, because in his heart he was trying hard to turn from that area of weakness.

JASON: I remember the moment I realized Rachid was my son. Until that day, I didn't understand how much I loved him.

He was a freshman in high school at Cumberland Christian, and they were barely two weeks into the school year. Rachid was trying to figure out how he fit in, and we knew he would have some rough patches. But my heart sank when my phone rang and they told me Rachid had been in a fight. I needed to come pick him up because he was suspended for two weeks.

Haley and I had known Rachid would struggle at times in this place that was so strange to him. But a fight at school? After just two weeks?

I pulled into the visitor's parking space and hurried inside. Rachid was sitting in a chair outside the principal's office with his head down.

"Rachid, what happened?" I said in a loud whisper.

He looked up and shook his head, but there was no time for an explanation.

We went into the principal's office, where the principal told me that Rachid had gotten into a fight playing basketball during a free period. Rachid did not look up or respond while they told me how he had picked up another boy and flipped him over on his back and started hitting him.

"Is that true, Rachid?" I asked. I couldn't believe he was unprovoked. I looked at him again and asked, "Why? What happened?"

He glanced up but did not look me in the eye. This is a cultural trait that Haley and I had come to understand, but other Americans did not. Children in Niger are told not to look adults in the eye. They don't shake hands with adults. They are completely subordinate. Now surrounded by adults, knowing he was in big trouble, Rachid withdrew even deeper into himself.

"Rachid, we can't help you if you won't let us," I said.

He kept his silence, and we had no choice but to go home.

I hoped that he might open up to me more when we were alone in the car, but he barely spoke, despite my pleadings.

"I want to support you," I told him when we got home, "but if you started this, I need to know. And if you didn't, I need to know that, too. I'll support you and I'll fight for you if I have to, but I need to know what happened."

Then he reached up and pulled his shirt away from his neck to reveal a bite wound on his shoulder. "This is why I hit him," he said softly.

Suddenly, I could feel anger and sadness to my core, and I wiped away tears. That was the moment I knew that Rachid was my son and I was his father. I loved him deeply. He had been hurt, and I was hurting for him.

When we got home, Rachid let Haley put antibiotic ointment on his shoulder, and he told us more of the story. During free period, he had been playing basketball with some senior boys. One of the older boys wanted the ball, and Rachid didn't want to give it up. The senior boy decided he would take it, and he pushed Rachid.

Well, Rachid was younger, but he was no weakling. He was strong, maybe stronger than the senior, and like I had heard in the principal's office, Rachid flipped the guy over on his back. That was when the senior pulled Rachid close to him and bit him hard on the shoulder—so hard he drew blood.

I told Rachid we needed go back to school the next day and explain.

Back in the principal's office again, I said, "Rachid, you need to share what you told me."

He pulled his shirt away to reveal the ugly bite. The principal immediately began to retreat and insisted that we could clear up the whole thing. He was backpedaling so fast, it was like he thought we might be planning to cause trouble for the school.

I assured him it was nothing like that . . . we just wanted everyone to know the whole story. A high school senior, who was the son of a teacher, appeared to have a lot more credibility than the new kid from Africa. The principal immediately dropped the suspension.

Since the time when Hunter and Pauline had been babies, Haley and I had dried their tears and bandaged their scrapes. We had held them and rocked them to sleep when they were afraid. We had loved them beyond anything they will ever imagine until they have their own children.

Rachid was a freshman in high school, on the verge of becoming a man. He was not crying now. Who had dried his tears as a child? Who had rocked him to sleep? Did he understand how much we loved him? Did we?

I believe the promise of Romans 8:28: "In all things God works for the good of those who love him, who have been called according to his purpose." Haley and I have seen sadness and pain in our visits to Niger, and we've seen God's miraculous work among the poorest. A school fight was a big deal to Haley and me, but compared to the pain Rachid had experienced in his life growing up in an orphanage? Not so much. Yet God took that opportunity to show me Rachid, my son. And God allowed me to show Rachid that we would have his back whenever he needed us.

HALEY: Endurance is "the ability to withstand hardship or adversity. Especially the ability to sustain a prolonged stressful effort or activity."[13]

When I think of the word *endurance,* my mind immediately pictures a person running a race. As they run, hills and obstacles block their way, but they have a determination within them to give it their all as they come around the corner and see the finish line. We as believers are running our own personal races with Jesus daily, and our finish line is eternity spent in heaven with our Savior.

We are all called to run different courses in life, whatever course the Lord has set before us. No matter the course or how many "obstacles" we must endure along the way, the question we must ask ourselves is, "Is it worth it?"

Am I running with the end prize in mind? Am I telling friends, family, and others how faithful my Jesus has been along the way? Am I telling of the miracles I have seen Him do? Am I sharing with others the prayers He has answered? Am I sharing with the lost that Jesus is worth it in the end? Have I shared that when my heart was shattered and broken to the point of constant aching, my only peace was Jesus? That is what we as believers are called to; to run our race well and to bring others across the finish line with us into eternity. That is the only reason we exist.

One of Jason's and my assignments during our race was God's calling to adopt Rachid. Adoption is a calling for sure and not for the weak. Bringing a person into your family who has a different DNA and has been brought up in a completely different culture brings many challenges that the entire family must work through. We, as a family, have learned to be patient. We have learned the art of truly listening and learning what another person's passion and viewpoint is like.

Rachid also endured incredibly well in his new country, his new culture, and his new school. He made all As and Bs, and at the end of the year Whitefield accepted him into the tenth grade, same as Hunter. He made the soccer team at Whitefield and continued his journey.

RACHID: When we played soccer in Niger, a group from our village would get together and look for an opponent to play. We didn't have a coach or anything. We just played anybody who would play against us. A crowd would gather to watch, and they would pick a team for the next game.

Playing for a coach was different. Having someone telling you to go here and do this. It wasn't every man for himself, like it was in Africa. When you get the ball you don't just try to dribble past everybody and score the goal. It's quick touch, quick touch, and release. I have to understand what to do to contribute to the team and win the game, not just try to score myself every time.

JASON: By the time Rachid was a junior in high school, we believed Rachid was strong enough to earn a soccer scholarship, so we created a web page with some of his game film. My friend Rich Matherne was taking his son, John, to a soccer camp at Messiah College in the Northeast, and he asked if I would like to attend the camp with Rachid. We went up, and at camp the players were all assigned randomly to one of thirteen coaches from other Christian colleges in the area for the entire camp. Rachid was placed with Coach Matt Horth from Gordon College in Massachusetts. After we returned home, the Gordon coach continued to stay in touch with us and Rachid. This was an interesting coincidence, because Haley's grandfather's name was Gordon, and she had gone to Gordon College in Barnesville, Georgia. We felt a sense of comfort that maybe the Lord was opening a door for Rachid.

HALEY: The coach came down to watch Rachid play, and he was impressed. He invited Rachid up for a tour of the college. Jason and I went up with him, and I was praying for confirmations along the way. The assistant head coach was showing us the facilities around campus, and the last place he took us was the athletic building. We walked up the stairs to the workout room, and painted on the back wall was Joshua 1:9, my life verse: "Have I not commanded you? Be strong and courageous. Do not be afraid; do not be discouraged, for the LORD your God will be with you wherever you go."

My eyes immediately filled with tears, and I knew this was the place the Lord had prepared for Rachid.

It wasn't going to be easy releasing him to the care of someone else. It had taken so long to work through the adoption process that we were only able to have Rachid in our home for a short time. That verse was a gift of peace for me, knowing that Rachid is in the Lord's care. His coaches are wonderful, godly Christian men who have invested in Rachid and all the players. This was definitely where the Lord wanted him to be.

Rachid has continued to endure and work very hard. Coming from a culture that does not naturally prioritize education, it is a miracle that Rachid has graduated from a college prep Christian high school and graduated from college in 2023. We are so proud of him and thankful for everyone who has supported Rachid in this journey!

During his senior year in high school, he wrote an essay and reflected back briefly on his childhood, around the time Jason and I would have met him for the first time. He wrote,

Becoming a Christian totally changed the course of my life and how I would treat others. I was seven to eight years old, living in the orphanage, when I accepted Christ Jesus into my heart. I always attended church with my friends that I grew up with in the orphanage, and all of them were saved as well. Hearing the name of God at church would always bring me joy. As a Christian I believed, and still believe, that there is only one God. The God I follow is the God almighty that created all things and made us in His own image. Therefore, with my faith in God, I believe that there is a purpose to my life and that my life has a meaning. I will take the opportunity of using the gifts that God has given me to glorify the Lord.

EIGHT

CALLED TO GET OUT OF YOUR COMFORT ZONE

JASON: I recently read a meme on the Internet that said, "Some things don't need prayer, they need discipline. God already told you what to do, you're just procrastinating." I don't like to seek comfort when I know I there are many things to be done to advance His kingdom. Praying is important, but so is acting. While our children were growing up through their teenage years, Haley and I continued our annual trips to Niger and continued to raise money for schools there. God showed up over and over, sometimes in miraculous ways.

After Dodgeball and the World Games, we began hosting a golf tournament at Eagle's Landing, and later we hosted a golf tournament in the spring and an event at Top Golf in the fall. We were looking for other ways to raise money for schools, and road races seemed like a natural fit. WinShape Foundation, created by Chick-fil-A founder Truett Cathy, and Connect Races were working with Chick-fil-A restaurant operators to put on races for marketing purposes. We proposed partnering with them to turn those races into fundraising opportunities for Schools for Niger, Africa (SFNA).

We partnered with Connect Races to put on a 5k and a one-mile fun run. We did the race for about four years, ending with a Nugget .9niner Family Fun Run held at Vinings Church. We had gotten pretty good at clearing anywhere from $25,000 to $40,000 for any of these events, and we averaged around $100,000 a year for SFNA across all our fundraising efforts.

We recruited more sponsors and topped out at about five hundred runners, and that generated about $30,000 per event. We also realized that there were leftover T-shirts from our races and from earlier ones that Connect had run. Over the years, we'd been storing hundreds of T-shirts in cardboard boxes. We couldn't let all those shirts sit in a warehouse, so we started taking them to Niger and giving them away. I still remember the first time we were out in the African bush and I saw a man wearing a Chick-fil-A T-shirt!

Wow, what a far-reaching influence we were having, not just the shirt the man wore but businessmen from Chick-fil-A visiting the poorest country in the world to share the good news of Jesus! This brought a tear to my eye.

Then there was the time when Brad, Lawson, and I took T-shirts to give to a group of Nigerien high schoolers at the Ebenezer School. We had a storage box filled with them, and a line of kids. Lawson was handing out T-shirts, and Brad started counting kids. He totaled 150.

I was standing off to the side when he came to me with a look of panic. "Jason, we don't have enough shirts," he said.

"Are you sure?" I asked. Because when you're handing out free stuff in Niger, you don't want to run out.

He said the two tubs had fewer than one hundred shirts, and there were a lot more kids than that.

Brad is a numbers guy, so I was confident that his numbers were correct.

"Well, if we run out, these kids are going to be upset, and the director of the school will be upset," I said. "We might have a serious issue."

Even as Lawson handed out shirt after shirt, more kids saw what was happening and ran over to join the line. Brad did a quick count of shirts to confirm the problem. And the kids kept coming.

And yet, somehow, every child got a shirt.

We all breathed a sigh of relief and a "thank you, God."

Later that night, we sat on the rooftop of the LINK Outreach Center reviewing the day and the episode. We hadn't been just five shirts short. We were way short. We hadn't misplaced a box that we found to save the day. The school was miles from our supplies, so nobody had brought out an extra box. In fact, this was the last school we visited— the last of the T-shirts we had brought over.

But every time Brad and Lawson reached into a tub, they came up with shirts.

Brad was literally in tears as he recounted the day. "I can honestly say that's the only miracle I know that I've witnessed in my life," he said. "We absolutely did not have enough T-shirts. They physically were not there. But God showed up. He really showed up."

HALEY: As a leader I always prayed for new opportunities for serving in Niger, and the Lord answered this prayer many times. Jesus told His followers to visit prisoners, and on a trip to Niger, the Lord provided a pastor's wife, Madame Ali, who took Jesus's words to heart. She visited the women's prison in Niamey every week. After she told me about her visits, I felt God encouraging me to take one of my mission teams into the prison.

I felt confident that I understood what God was calling me to do and knew that He would have to make it happen. Getting government approval would not be easy. The prison normally did not allow groups larger than four, and there would be twelve of us. But a week before we left the US, Edem called and said we had been approved. God's hand was with us.

I reached out to Edem and asked if there was anything we could provide for the ladies in the prison. Edem contacted the prison warden, and in a few days Edem got back to me with the answer: soap. I asked him to clarify: bars of soap or liquid soap? While waiting for Edem's answer, one of my team members told me she had a friend who worked at a hotel and they had several hundred bars of soap they were getting rid of. Would we like them? I immediately said yes, knowing that this was the Lord's provision for what Edem was going to tell me they needed.

Edem called a few days later and confirmed it was bars of soap that the inmates needed.

These stories happened over and over throughout my years of leading teams. The Lord knew what we needed before we even asked. I filled a fourteen-gallon Rubbermaid storage tub with bars of soap for the prisoners—a simple gift that could make a real difference in the way they felt every day.

Let me say here that I love to study the Bible and all the great characters in it. I am specifically inspired by the shepherd boy David, one of my favorite people in the Bible. David became a great leader for the Lord. He was a man after God's own heart, yet when he was chosen to be Israel's king, he was young, inexperienced—teachable and eager.

I relate to David in many ways. I truly want to be a woman after God's own heart. I was inexperienced when I first led a team, yet I had passion and was eager to learn.

The Lord was so gracious to me in my failures, mistakes, valleys, and mountaintop experiences, and He has grown my faith through it all. Leading a group of people in a fourth-world country is a huge responsibility and one I never took lightly.

As a king, David also was a brave warrior for the Lord. He would seek the Lord and His direction and then David obeyed. Leading teams in Niger also requires bravery at times. I remember a few times that the Lord called me to respond with bravery, especially on this trip into the women's prison.

The day before our visit to the prison, I explained to the ladies as much as I knew about what we might experience. Most were excited. A few were worried. They asked a lot of questions, and I could only say, "I don't know. This is our first time. But here's what I do know: God has made a way for each one of us to get in. So there's a plan and there's a purpose for us to visit inside this prison."

Madame Ali was with us. If we were going to be able to build a relationship with these ladies, she would be the key.

Guards met us at the gate with rifles over their shoulder. The men who would protect us seemed very intimidating. They wanted to know what was in the tub.

"Soap," I said, and I lifted the lid so they could see. They shuffled the bars around to make sure we hadn't hidden anything underneath, then said they would take it.

"No," I said. "We have permission to distribute it."

"We will do that," they insisted. (Madame Ali was translating for us.)

That wasn't going to happen. The Lord had made it clear to me that we were to give this soap to the prisoners in the name and with the love of Jesus.

"No," I said. "We will take it in."

These men were obviously not accustomed to being told no by a woman, and the tension rose. In that moment, God gave the courage of David and reminded me that this soap was the Lord's provision. We were His deliverers. I looked them in the eye, shook my finger, and said, respectfully, "You will not take our soap. We have approval, and we will be distributing it, or it will not be distributed at all."

The guards backed away and opened the gate for us.

Entering the prison was intimidating to say the least. My ladies were watching me to see how I would respond, and I reassured them, "It's going to be okay. God has us!" I was whispering these same words to myself over and over as we walked through this unnerving process.

We entered one gate, and it was locked behind us. Then we entered a second gate, and then it, too, was locked. Many of the inmates were staring at us, wondering why we were there. I told my team, "Keep walking and smiling. God is with us."

We made our way up a steep, winding, spiral staircase, dark and musty smelling, passing several armed guards on our way to the warden's office. After we spoke with him for twenty minutes and explained what we would be sharing with the ladies in prison and assured him our hearts were to educate and love the ladies in the prison, he gave us his blessing.

We made our way back down the winding staircase, and all eyes were on us as we passed through one last gate. We could hear the women on the other side of the walls speaking their tribal languages. At this point I knew I had some team members who were excited and some who were not so thrilled to be there. I kept encouraging them to get out of their comfort zone, which is something we often talked about on these mission trips.

In a room with the prisoners, we sang songs and danced. Some of the women came over and began dancing and singing with us while others stood back and watched. Then we shared a Bible story, and while we were telling the story, things began falling off ledges within the concrete walls. Plastic bottles and other items the ladies had placed on the walls randomly fell to the floor.

Once again, my ladies looked at me, and I calmly reminded them Satan was trying to distract the ladies in the prison from hearing the good news of the gospel. "Keep on reading," I said.

Then we handed out buckets, wash cloths, soap, candy, and other items we had brought. Several prisoners asked us to pray with them. One shared that she was a Christian and asked if we could get her a Bible.

This is what it was all about. She made all the intimidation worth it. No wonder the bottles were falling off the wall! Satan was working hard trying to keep the ladies in prison from hearing the truth of how much Jesus loves them. We had prayed that while we were there spending time with these ladies that they would see something different in us. That they would experience Jesus and be drawn to the light, His light in us.

As we were making our way back through the gates and heading back to our van, many of the ladies said this experience was one of their favorites. I smiled and thanked the Lord for His protection and goodness of what our team had the privilege to experience behind those scary, intimidating concrete walls!

We visited a women's prison every year after that, and when we returned to one we'd visited before, the women cheered as we came through the doors. They knew we cared about them and loved them.

We still had moments of fear, like the time the power went out when we were in the warden's office with no windows. The room immediately went black, and my team members were all reaching for their phones to get some light. The situation lasted for only a minute, but it was a long minute with twelve women, the warden, and the guard, both of them armed.

It truly was a walk by faith. Praying for confirmation gave me peace that the Lord had already opened the doors, and His plans were to prosper us and not to harm us. I had to coach myself and then remind my girls of that, and I hoped we would always be open and unafraid of the next adventure. He calls us to visit the prisoners, wherever they may be.

JASON: Haley's experiences in the women's prisons encouraged me to schedule a similar visit for a men's team I was leading. We had a very different experience.

The night before I took the guys into a prison for the first time, I told them about the plan. I had not put it on the itinerary for the week, so they were learning about it for the first time.

"My wife would not go for this," one of my friends confided.

"You might wait and tell her about it later," I said.

I knew several of the guys were nervous, but like Haley, I believed God was guiding us and would protect us. Pastor Ali visited the men in the prison often and was building relationships. I also knew LINK Missions would not have supported our visit if they believed our safety was at risk.

The next morning twelve of us stood inside the prison grounds, in an outdoor space about twenty by thirty feet surrounded by a thirty-foot-high wall. The sun was already turning the space into an outdoor oven, and flies were buzzing. A bit of roof, more like an overhang, extended from one of the walls and provided the only shade. Dirty mats were laid out under the overhang for the men to sit.

A door opened, and twenty prisoners entered the space. Like Haley's group visiting the women, we immediately felt the angry stares. We looked around at the walls and the two doors—one led to the outside, the prisoners were coming through the other one. It felt like we were in a movie, but this was real life.

In that situation, most men go into defense mode in their minds, and I felt my group going there. *How am I going to protect myself? What if a brawl erupts?* The door closed and locked behind the prisoners. There was only one guard to help, and he stood close to the door. *How will we get out of here? The walls are thirty feet high.*

The men were so close, and they smelled so bad. They all were either barefoot or wore torn-up flip-flops. Dirt and grime were ground into their feet and hands. I began to imagine the hard life they lived and prayed for the right words to say to them. This place and the hardship these men faced was unimaginable. Did they have any hope at all?

We visited with them and prayed for them and spoke of Jesus, and for several of the men, our prayers seemed only to intensify the hate in their eyes. Unlike Haley and the women, we knew these men did not want us to perform a skit or throw our arms around them and dance with them. Lawson Bailey said afterward, "I felt like I wasn't looking at someone who hated me. I was looking at something in them that hated Jesus in me—like spiritual warfare."

God had led us to this place, and we were part of His plan for these men. But when we left, we still did not know how He might use our visit, but we didn't give up on visiting prisons.

A couple of years later, I was planning for an upcoming mission and confirming what supplies we would need to pack. Edem and I had emailed each other back and forth several times to discuss a prison visit. We had discussed us bringing soap, T-shirts, bowls for them to eat out of, and possibly toys. I asked him in a reply email what age they were, and he said fourteen to twenty years old.

I told him I wasn't sure what kind of toys we would bring. Edem needed to know soon, so he could report everything that we would be taking into the prison. In the meantime, I was cleaning out the storage space at my Vinings Chick-fil-A, and I found a bag with eight Frisbees in it. Cara suggested I give them away to employees.

I said, "Hmm, no, I'll take these to Niger."

That day I took them home and dropped them in a tub in my garage. The next morning, I woke up to an email from Edem saying the toys we *need* to bring to the prison should be Frisbees! What? *Go, God!* The boys loved the Frisbees, and we played with them for more than thirty minutes when we arrived. Later that day, twenty-nine of the boys raised their hands to accept Christ! "I [Jesus] tell you that in the same way there will be more rejoicing in heaven over one sinner who repents than over ninety-nine righteous persons who do not need to repent" (Luke 15:7).

Other Nigerien adventures have been more fun and sometimes more dangerous than we considered at the time. When I climbed into the little boat at the edge of the Niger River, I was excited about the possibility of seeing a hippopotamus up close. Two more guys joined me, and our guide and his helper pushed the little boat into the water. We immediately began to rock, and I grabbed the sides of the boat to settle myself. This was not the type of boat or the type of water I was hoping to be "called out of" by Jesus; no, these were muddy unknown waters.

Now, when I say "boat," I'm using the term loosely. We were in what's known as a *pirogue*, a dugout canoe from a single tree trunk. The unsteadiness was to be expected. What

I didn't expect was for water to be leaking into the boat from the bottom. While our guide used a pole to propel the little boat forward, his helper bailed water with a small bucket.

The river was swift, and our guide was adept at keeping us on course toward a hippo upstream.

I must have made that trip ten times, and Haley did the same on her trips, taking women with her out into the Niger River. When I think back on that, it might have been the craziest thing we did in Africa. But I had learned to trust God and His promise of protection over our team and any team Haley had led. Other situations were potentially more dangerous, but this excursion was for the pure adventure of it—to see one of God's massive creatures up close. And we did. One of those giant hippos would open his mouth so wide, you could count his big teeth.

You'd think (or, at least we thought) that because hippos are herbivores, they wouldn't be a danger to people. In fact, they are one of the most dangerous mammals in Africa, accounting for more human deaths and attacks than any other. They are very territorial and will attack boats or people or crocodiles or anything else that gets too close. Water is their home, and they swim faster than you can imagine.

Men who rely on the river for their livelihood, either as fishermen or ferrymen or guides for tourists like us, learn how to avoid close contact with the hippos. But they must get into the water to survive, and each trip risks attack.

Due to the risk, LINK stopped trying to recreate that aspect of a true Niger experience. The risk was too great simply for the adventure of it. Then in 2014, a hippo attacked and overturned a boat near Niamey carrying children across the river to school. Twelve children and one adult died. They were not looking for adventure, just living their lives.

God is with us every step we take. On a mission in 2013 we attended a church service, and local missionary Beki Rohan was our translator. The whole team wore headsets, and Beki would translate what was being said, in either French or a local tribal language, back to the team.

I was asked to introduce the team, so I did so and then sat back down. Rodrigo turned to me and said, "They are expecting you to give the message this morning."

"Ha, you are funny!" I responded.

Beki then translated through the headset, "Is someone on the team prepared to give a message this morning?"

This had never happened before. Even though there must have been a breakdown in communication before we got there, I was the leader and knew I could not ask anyone else to step up on this short of notice. So I stood up and began to walk forward, clutching my Bible and praying that God would give me a sermon in the ten or twelve remaining steps I had before being on stage.

My favorite Bible to carry is the John Maxwell Leadership Bible, and that is what I had with me that morning. I turned to Nehemiah, and with the help of God and John Maxwell, I delivered a twenty-minute sermon. Of course, it didn't hurt that the message had to be translated into two different languages, and while they did this, I was able to prepare for what I was to say next.

The next year, I prepared just in case I needed to deliver a message last minute again. I was up until midnight, and God laid on my heart the verse Matthew 28:19: "Therefore go and make disciples of all nations, baptizing them in the name of the Father and of the Son and of the Holy Spirit." I shared it with Carter Tucker, one of the team members on the mission.

When we arrived at church the next day, we learned that the pastor did not expect or need anyone to deliver a message. In fact, he had a special message he wanted to share with the whole church. The pastor opened his Bible and began reading the very verse I'd shared with Carter the night before, Matthew 28:19! Are you kidding me? Carter and I looked at each other immediately with wide eyes and open mouths. I leaned over to him and whispered, "God, we hear You, are You really this close to us?"

God whispered to us that day!

HALEY: I remember bringing some of the youth teams over and we decided to bring reusable diapers to the moms of children under two years old in a remote village several hours outside of the city. This was an eye-opening experience for the students. We educated the moms and demonstrated how to use the diapers before we began the distribution process. When we began we had enough diapers for the children who were in line, but after the word began to get out the moms kept coming. There were a few times in Niger when we as a team were providing items and the Nigeriens would become so afraid that they wouldn't receive the item that it turned into a free-for-all. Our local translators would explain to them to be patient and stay in line and that we would get the items to them, but sometimes we would have to "close up shop" to avoid total chaos. I was used to the overwhelming process from serving so many times in Niger, but this shook some of the younger team members. I truly believe the Lord gave me a different mindset while serving on the mission field. I can remember being afraid only a few times during my many years of serving in Niger. I was confident in the God I served and believed that the God of Abraham, Isaac, and Jacob was the same God who was with me every time I stepped out of the boat to walk on water with Him.

JASON: We don't want to own schools, and we don't want to run schools, but we also don't want to be a grant-writing organization that just hands out money to partners running schools. We want to change how education happens at

Christian schools in Niger. We want to make sure that they have a building that is safe and that they are getting the proper curriculum to learn. We also want to make sure that Jesus is being shared and that the teachers are Christians. Students should learn about the kingdom of God and how they might change Niger in the future.

A lot of organizations want to control the whole operation. It's their way or the highway. Others simply write checks and send money. We take the position that this school belongs to our Christian partners in Niger and we will help, but we do want them to meet certain expectations for us to continue to support them.

I took a team to Niger just before COVID shut down international travel, and I was disappointed to see the condition of a school we had built a few years earlier. It was in bad need of repair, and there was trash all over the grounds. It clearly had not been maintained. I left that day more convinced than ever that we need to be clear about our expectations for excellence in the schools we build and support, and an important part of that messaging is in our willingness to build model schools.

I understand the need for cultural sensitivity, but excellence is not uniquely American. My dad taught me, and then Chick-fil-A reinforced in me, the importance of doing things right. At Chick-fil-A, we refer to "the two crucial pickles." When we make a Chick-fil-A chicken sandwich, we spread the pickles out so that every time you take a bite, you get a little taste of pickle. If they were stacked on top of each other, it wouldn't be the same experience. Some might think that's a minor detail, but our customers would immediately taste the difference.

Of course, when I see all the trash around the school, I remind myself that there is no trash pickup in Niger. Trash is everywhere, not just around the schools. And yet I remembered the school visited years earlier that had been built with tile on every wall and floor. They have fewer students than other schools, so the quality of instruction for each student was higher. If eighteen kids are in one classroom learning the gospel along with math and science, and seventy kids are in another classroom sitting four to a desk, I'm convinced the eighteen will have better outcomes.

I'm not looking to simply spend more money but to create a standard of excellence that our school directors can see is achievable. This is what we expect in our school buildings and in our teachers and our students.

HALEY: We know the directors are trying to maintain a certain level of quality and cleanliness in their schools in Niger, and that can be so difficult. From the very first time I visited Niger, it was overwhelming to observe the large amounts of trash everywhere. Niger didn't have any trash service. When people drink a bag of water in Niamey, they just throw the bag on the ground. Everybody does it. That's what the children experience every day, so we're trying to create a whole new mindset, which is a huge feat. It's the right thing to do to set the bar higher, but we have to be realistic about our expectations. If parents aren't going to make kids pick up around their homes, then why would they expect that when they come to school? How do we raise the expectations? That's what we want to do, and that's part of what we believe God is calling us to do.

JASON AND HALEY: We as Christians shouldn't seek comfort. If you truly want to walk on water, the only way to do so is by keeping your eyes fixed on Jesus. Oh, and you have to get out of the boat too!

NINE

CALLED TO OBEDIENCE

JASON: My dad would always say to me, "If you are going to do something don't do it halfway!" I was taught at Chick-fil-A as a new team member to do things right the first time. Obedience was instilled in me at an early age. In his book *In a Pit with a Lion on a Snowy Day*, Mark Batterson says, "Obedience is a willingness to do whatever, whenever, wherever God calls us."[14] Haley and I could have written the whole Rachid adoption story under this chapter, as a sign of ultimate obedience and trust in the Lord, but we felt it deserved its own space in a previous chapter. Someone once shared with me that so many people are waiting to be called to do missions or share the gospel with others. But good news! God has already called everyone in Matthew 28:19, also known as the Great Commission: "Therefore go and make disciples of all nations, baptizing them in the name of the Father and of the Son and of the Holy Spirit."

HALEY: Paulina was a junior in high school when she heard God's call to Africa. We had taken the children as part of a two-week-long youth mission from Whitefield, but God was calling her to spend an extended stay. Jason and I prayed and sought God's guidance, and He gave us peace.

My heart was thrilled for Paulina—for her desire to serve God in this way and for the opportunity to stay in Niger for an entire month. I was not worried about her staying in the country at all. She would be with Beki and Jeremy (the rock star we mentioned earlier). The concern for me as her mom was her flying by herself from Atlanta through Paris into Niamey.

PAULINA: A lot of people in the United States guard their children so much they wouldn't think of letting them leave the country alone. They think it's too dangerous. Because my mom and dad had gone to Niger themselves, they widened my horizon to do whatever God wants me to do. That's a big blessing for me. I'm honored to have grown up in a household where my parents have always supported missions, going overseas, the Great Commission, and the sacrifice that comes with that. This perspective in our family has helped develop my call and view of what it looks like to go overseas on missions, for which I am eternally grateful.

At the same time, my parents are called to live here in the United States. My calling is different, and it came from going over and living with the missionaries and seeing what they were doing for Christ in Africa. Day by day, God created a new desire within me.

A month in Africa was so different from a weeklong mission trip. My time there was more aligned with the rhythm of day-to-day life, and that was really eye-opening. On a mission trip, with a limited number of days, you want to cram all the good experiences you can into those days. Living there for a month, day in and day out, we didn't try to do so much every day. Instead, we might walk to the market one day and buy our vegetables, then walk back and prepare the meal. And that's what we would do that day. Some days were exciting, but mostly it was living the reality of life in Niger, and I was so thankful for that experience. Anybody who believes the Lord has called them to the mission field should do something like that first.

I shadowed three different missionaries while I was in Niger. Joel was working at CURE Hospital and was a professional storyteller. He was awesome with children. He took pictures of the kids during their stay at the hospital for surgery. He met them before their surgery and learned about them, then he wrote their stories and put them on their blogs to share with people who might want to help the children pay for their treatment. Donors could see the impact of their generosity. That work was so inspiring.

Another missionary friend of ours, Hope, worked with children with special needs. She took me to different villages, and we went into the huts where the children lived to visit with them.

There was a seventeen-year-old boy, my age at the time, and he was so small. He wasn't verbal. He just screamed with excitement when he saw me. He wanted me to hold him, so I did. I picked him up, and he wrapped his arms around me like a spider and just screamed with joy. When it was time to leave, he wouldn't let me go. It was so hard to pull away from him. That boy, seventeen years old, so full of joy while I was there, was living his life out in a tiny hut. What would become of him? Some families leave their children with physical or developmental issues in the huts for hours because they're ashamed of them. Like Hope, I left that day inspired to find a way to help children with special needs.

Another missionary, Beki, used sports activities to bring people in and share the gospel with them. Even though I'm not as interested in sports as my brothers and my father, I was interested to see how many different ways these missionaries connected with people.

When we walked the streets of Niger, we were often the only white faces in the crowd, and that was a new experience for me. There were days when I just wanted to blend in with everybody. In America, of course, when we walk down the street we see people of many races, and the differences don't seem so different. Everybody blends in. To live for years at a time in a place where you stand out so clearly because of the way you look could be difficult, I'm sure.

I also went to prayer meetings where the people were all praying in different languages, like in the book of Acts. Then other days, like I said, were quieter. One missionary couple had a one-year-old baby, and I was her "sister" for a month, helping them take care of her. I couldn't imagine what it was like for her growing up in this country where I was a visitor. I watched how they were parenting her and saw all of that in the context of my call to mission work. The experience was both inspiring and eye-opening.

HALEY: Paulina's trip was a taste for us of what her life and future would look like as a missionary. We felt like this was a "first small step," which would continue to strengthen our trust in the Lord and remind us that He has Paulina in His hands and loves her more than we do.

It was also a great reminder for us that we have no control over what happens to our children or our own lives while here on this earth. We surrender that control to the Lord and say, "It is well with our souls," whatever He wills for our lives and the lives of our children.

It brings to my mind Proverbs 16:9: "In their hearts humans plan their course, but the LORD establishes their steps."

Though we were confident in the Lord's protection, we also stayed in touch with Paulina, especially as she traveled from Atlanta to Paris (trying to navigate Charles de Gaulle airport, which is a very confusing airport) to Niamey, where she would be met by our friends.

I'm still a mom, and I didn't sleep much that night as Paulina called me when she landed in Paris and again when an Air France employee took her to a room to wait until it was time for her next flight. After another five-and-a-half-hour flight and another hour to get through customs, Beki texted a photo of Paulina in Niger, and I was relieved.

Trusting God never means we are not concerned, especially for our children, or that we are reckless. Paulina communicated with us at the end of each day she was in Niger, so we had the peace and assurance that she was good, safe, healthy, and happy.

PAULINA: You can't just come into another country and share the gospel and expect people to accept it. You have to build relationships, and that takes time. Sometimes children might accept what you're telling them, but a lot of the older men and women see the world outside of their faith as evil, and you have to show them over time that, actually, you love them.

The professional storyteller I met told me to get into a kid's story. Hear their heart and what they've been through. Live with them. Be with them. Jesus said, "Abide in me." You have to show them that you're not going to leave, but that you're there to be part of their community and to love them. That's when you start opening up a little bit more, and then you see an opportunity to share the gospel.

Loving Rachid and knowing he has siblings back in Niger is a big reason I feel called to mission work full time. I don't want to just go over there, wherever "there" is, and help people and then come back. I want to live there with them. If God calls me to, I would love to start a foundation or an orphanage where I can take children in—not just a regular orphanage where they have to leave at a certain age, but where they're provided with a home and a person they can call mom and dad, and a place where they can know Christ. I don't necessarily want to bring children to the States or leave them behind when I come back, but I would rather go live with them and be with them and love them there in their country.

JASON: I have to admit, I was not a fan of our only daughter going to a fourth-world country for a month without us, even though it was Niger and we had been many times before. You see, those other times, I, Paulina's earthly father, was there to protect her, and I was not ready to trust her total safety and well-being to her Heavenly Father. Wow, did I really admit that in writing? I guess I am human and have struggled with this whole idea of obedience. Don't get me wrong, I knew that Paulina was being called to the mission field, but not this early. Come on, God, let me have my little blue-eyed girl a little longer.

Obedience starts with trust, and I had been gifted at developing leaders at Chick-fil-A who I trusted to run my business. I trusted God to take care of me and even my wife, Haley, while in Niger, so why not this time? I had been working and praying for the Lord to send laborers into His harvest, but this was different. It was our daughter. I will say there was never a moment that I felt fully at peace with this decision to support her trip, but I decided to let go and trust God. I prayed, *Lord, I pray You will expand my vision of a lost world and break my heart to support all those who spread the gospel to those whose souls starve for salvation from Jesus. Even my only daughter. Amen.*

This whole idea of being obedient to what God has planned for us can be hard and scary at times. Warren Weirsbe, in his book *On Being a Servant of God*, said, "It's not ability God is looking for but availability."[15] My prayer for you and my prayer for me is that we will always answer God's call so that we may enjoy the fruits of it.

PAULINA: I think the moment we choose to follow the Lord, that's when we surrender—or we should surrender—our whole lives to Him. And I think it's not just those who go out in mission work, but every follower of Christ should be surrendering their whole life to Him, whether He calls you to stay here and minister in the dentist's office or He's given you a heart for another culture to go overseas. I have given my whole life to follow Christ, but it doesn't seem like a burden for me to go overseas. It's like when you talk to a nursing student and they tell you, "I can't imagine doing anything else!" It's the same for me. I cannot imagine doing anything else with my life than going over to Niger. I honestly see it as such a gift and a joy that my job is to share Christ with every person I come in contact with. What kind of job is that? And we all have that job, we all have that burden, but I get to go and give my life to the Lord in that way.

I don't know what that will look like for me—if He'll call me to be a nurse or a teacher or something else—but I see it as a joy and the best job that I could ever take on. There is a weight that comes with that. Some of my friends also very much want to be international missionaries, and we cry together at times because we'll have to say goodbye to our families one day for a long period of time. They may not get to see our kids grow up for a while. We can't date certain people because they don't want to go overseas. That has been one of the biggest sacrifices I have seen in my life.

But I count it all loss for the sake of Christ. If we aren't all feeling that burden at times, if we aren't feeling that loss at times, then I don't know if we're surrendered fully to the Lord and what He has called us to do.

HUNTER: As Christians, we need to constantly remind ourselves of our daily submission to the Lord. I'm not in charge, and my life isn't mine. I submit to the Lord and His authority, and my plans can change. I want to find a way to pour out and serve and use my resources to give back to those less fortunate than me, whether that's overseas or here. At least for the short term, I will pray for where God wants me to serve.

Once I move out on the road and join the Leadership Development Program with Chick-fil-A, I'll have a better idea of what I'll do with my life, but I definitely want to find some way to pour out my love for God. For now, I'll continue just living with open hands and saying, "Hey, Lord, if You want me to do something else in a couple years, that's Your will." And that's His call. Every day it's a submission and saying, "Lord, I'm here for You. My life is Your life; I give You the pen, and You write the story. I trust You wherever You call me to."

TEN

CALLED TO SURRENDER

HALEY: S·U·R·R·E·N·D·E·R

One of the things I looked forward to every year was the "word activity" that we did as a team on our trips to Niger.

The idea was to allow God to give a word to each of us by speaking through the prayers of someone else. To make sure it was God's word and not our friend's word for us, we kept our names hidden.

We each wrote our name on a piece of paper, folded it, and placed it in a bowl. Then everyone drew out a name but did not look at it. Instead, they just hid it away to pull back out later, or I offered to keep them for anyone who thought they might be too curious. I'd write their name on the outside and hide it.

We did this on the first evening of the mission. Then each of us began praying that the Lord would give us a specific word for the person whose name we had drawn.

On our second night of a mission on the rooftop, after we'd shared our highs and lows from the day, I asked if God had revealed to anyone the word for their person. It was still

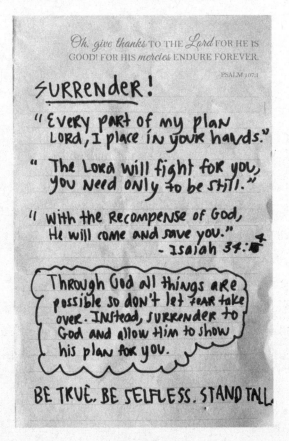

early in the week, but to some the Lord had already revealed a word. That woman would say the word, then share how the Lord had revealed it to her. Then she would unfold the paper and read the name of the person the word was for. Sometimes the person receiving the word would know it was for her even before her name was read, and that was such a powerful moment.

The first time I participated in this activity I was skeptical and unsure. I felt pressure that the Lord might not give me a word for this person by the time the mission was over. As always, though, when we truly seek the Lord, we will find Him. He spoke through Scripture, a story, in prayer, or through an experience with our friends in Niger. He always provided a word for me to share with the person whom I had been praying for.

This was a powerful process to participate in. To be the one praying for someone and to receive the word the Lord had given that person was always reassuring—a reminder that He hears us and will answer us if we are willing to hear Him.

Whenever my name was drawn, I was anxious and excited to hear my word. Every year that the Lord used this activity to reveal to me a word, He would then show me over and over throughout that year why He had given that particular word to me.

In June 2019, I was leading a youth team, and one night on the rooftop under the stars, Ellie, one of our team members, spoke the word *surrender*. That was an interesting word in this place. Everyone in the group had made sacrifices to be in this place to serve His children with love. What was the Lord asking someone to surrender?

Ellie shared some of the specific thoughts God had given to her about surrender:

- "Every part of my plan, Lord, I place in Your hands."
- "The LORD will fight for you; you need only to be still" (Exod. 14:14).
- "Through God all things are possible, so don't let fear take over. Instead, surrender to God and allow Him to show His plan for you."

As she explained how the Lord had given her the word, I continued to wonder who it might be for. Then she unfolded her paper, looked directly at me, and said, "Haley."

Me? Surrender? I was surprised and a little perplexed. I had surrendered my life to Jesus, and I had surrendered my plans to Him. So, what was He asking of me by giving me this word?

Ellie had written the word, along with her notes, on white journaling paper, so I took it home and hung it above my desk so I would see and read it often. I did not know then that this would be the last word that I would receive on a mission to Niger, and I had no idea how much I would be tested in this area of my life.

The pandemic hit and shut the world down beginning in March 2020. I was scheduled to lead a trip to Niger in October 2020, but international travel was discontinued. My heart was broken as this was the first time in twelve years that I would not be able to travel to Niger with a team to serve on the mission field. Oh, my heart was heavy, and I missed the people of Niger so much. Yet I understood the world was still shut down and I could do nothing to change this outcome.

In November 2020, some travel restrictions began to be lifted, and I told Jason that I really wanted to go to Niger and check on our friends and organizations we had built relationships with over the years. No teams had been able to visit Niger since February. Jason was hesitant to take this trip because of the unknown. What if we tested positive for COVID-19 and had to quarantine in Niger for another ten to fourteen days at the end of the mission when he needed to be back at work?

After several months of me asking him to go, he agreed that we would go together. Just the two of us would make our way to Niger in January 2021. We had many obstacles and challenges to overcome, but the Lord made a way for us to return. Our PCR tests came back in time and were negative. We were able to pack supplies and bring those items with us. It was such a precious time for Jason and me. In all our years of ministry, we had traveled to Niger only four times together. This would be the first time he and I would be doing ministry alone together. I planned as though I were traveling with a regular team. We had a Bible story to share with the children, we had supplies to hand out at the different locations we were going to visit, and the Lord really blessed this special time together.

However, a mission is never complete without some kind of spiritual warfare. As Jason mentioned earlier in the book, he became extremely ill the second day we were in Niger. He looked at me at lunchtime as we were making our way back to the compound where we were staying and said, "Haley, I just don't feel right." When we arrived, he went and laid down. That afternoon I went outside and was journaling and talking with some of the staff, then later that afternoon, around 4 o'clock, I went in to check on him and I remember him telling me, "Haley, I have never been this sick."

I called one of our missionary friends who we had known for many years and asked him to come by when he could. He came by later that evening and saw how sick Jason was and offered to drive us to a Christian clinic nearby.

An American doctor had started the clinic and had trained Nigerien doctors and nurses to operate it. I had visited another clinic on a previous mission, so I knew not to expect the modern equipment or the quickness of service we might have experienced at home.

When we arrived, Jason was so sick he could barely hold himself up. I was praying to God to please, please pull Jason through whatever he was experiencing. If we had been at home, I might have taken a minute to call Cheryl, who would have immediately started a prayer chain. Now it was just my prayers God heard. And He did hear my prayers. After only a few minutes they called Jason back to the examination room, and after several tests they determined he had food poisoning. Praise God! After a day and a half, thankfully, Jason was able to rejoin me, and we finished the mission together.

After not being able to visit Niger in 2020, I tried to absorb everything I could on this January 2021 mission, realizing that it was not guaranteed that we would be able to return every year.

On one of the days of this mission, Jason was visiting schools, and I took the opportunity to go for a long walk with Lucia Eberle, who had been a missionary in Niger for twenty-five years. Her parents had also been missionaries.

Leading teams to Niger through the years, I had never had the opportunity for a slow day like this. We walked down to the river, and she spoke to people she knew along the way. I was taking photographs of Niger up close and slow. It was such a beautiful experience. When we reached the river, a group of women were in the water washing their laundry. We talked with them for a bit, and then I asked if I could take their picture. They shook their heads and said no, and that was fine. I wanted them to know I respected their privacy. Lucia and I talked with them a little longer, then turned to leave. A minute later, one of the women called us back and asked Lucia about the photos we might take. She said I wouldn't photograph their faces; I just wanted to show my friends back home the beauty of Niger and a bit of what everyday life was like.

So that's how it started, and within a few minutes we were taking selfies and videos together, dancing and laughing. It was one of my sweetest moments in Niger.

Walking back, Lucia was excited because she had seen that group of women many times, but that was the first time the Lord had created an opportunity for her to engage with them. She also told me about a micro-business ministry her mother had started for widows in Niger and two neighboring countries. We visited three of the widows in their homes and prayed with them, and I could feel the presence of the Lord in that moment. I began to sense that He might be calling me to minister to widows in some way as well.

I shed many tears and held many friends very close as our time came to an end in the country I loved so much. My heart was so grateful that Jason and I had been privileged to travel together during a worldwide pandemic to see these people we cared so much about halfway around the world. In my heart, I wondered if I would ever be able to return to this place that held such a special place in my heart. Just as "Mary treasured up all these things and pondered them in her heart" (Luke 2:19), so did I.

The world continued to be shut down with the COVID-19 pandemic in 2021 with certain travel restrictions. However, it looked as though I would be able to take a small group of ladies over to Niger in June of that year. My heart was overjoyed! Over time people had donated lots of reusable diapers, clothing, and other supplies for me to take, so I felt obligated to get to Niger as soon as possible.

The PCR testing would still be in place, and if any of the travelers tested positive before leaving Niger, that person would have to remain in Niger for ten days or until they tested negative. We were all willing to take this risk to be able to spend time with the people of Niger and share the gospel with those who desperately needed to hear God's truth. We moved forward and paid our airfare, packed supplies in tubs, and felt the excitement building among the team.

Then, as the Lord would allow, new restrictions were implemented in April 2021 that prevented our team from traveling to Niger. My heart shattered into a million pieces. *How could this happen, Lord? We were going to serve Your people and to love on our dear friends whom we missed so much.* I experienced despair like I have never felt in my life. My heart was truly broken—that's the only way I can describe the pain that I felt. It went into the depths of my bones and into my soul, and all I could do was cry, "I don't understand, Lord. I am serving You. So why would You take this from me?"

Devastation, withdrawal, heartbreak, grief, these were all the emotions that I continued to feel days after this news had been shared with me.

Then one afternoon I sat at my desk and looked up at the word hanging in front of me: *surrender*.

I read the note Ellie had written, words God had spoken to her for me: "Through God all things are possible, so don't let fear take over. Instead, surrender to God and allow Him to show His plan for you." And, "Every part of my plan, Lord, I place in Your hands."

Was God asking me to surrender my plans for serving His children in Niger?

I was feeling completely lost, even as I prayed for His comfort.

Jason had never seen me like this, and he didn't know how to help me or what he could do to ease my pain. But Jason is a problem-solver by nature, especially where our children and I are concerned. He couldn't bear to see me this way, so without me knowing, he called some missionary friends of ours, Juanita and Rodrigo Rivas, whom we used to serve with in Niger. They were now living and serving in Alaska. Jason explained the situation to them—that I was supposed to be taking a small team to Niger and now could not—and asked if they would be willing to host us instead.

The Rivases shared with Jason that they had been praying that God would send them a team, but they had no idea where it would come from. We were now an answer to the prayers they had been praying. Only God!

Jason also asked them if they had any idea what the group could do there in Alaska. Rodrigo replied, "There are some widows who could use some help."

Jason told Rodrigo that he would talk to me and get back to him. He prayed for me and continued to ask God if this might be the right opportunity. Then a few days later he told me, "Haley, would you please just hear me out? Don't say no until you've heard all the details."

Well, that's an interesting way to begin a conversation. So I listened, and he shared with me how he had called Rodrigo and Juanita. He said they were willing to host my team and that Rodrigo said we could work with widows.

Before I could speak, I started crying as the Lord reminded me of the widows I had met on our last trip to Niger. Now it seemed as if the Lord might be giving me an opportunity to continue working with widows in the future. And that was the one thing Rodrigo mentioned. Only God!

I didn't want to give him my answer out of my emotion. Instead, I said I would pray about it and let him know. I prayed about the mission to Alaska, asking God if this is what He wanted for me at this time. I was still grieving and dealing with the loss of opportunity in Niger. When I fully accepted that the mission to Niger was not going to happen, I was in such a dark and lonely place, I knew the only one who could heal my heart was Jesus. In James we are told we will face trials in this life; however, this was not one I ever saw coming! With confusion and pain consuming me, I opened my Bible and asked the Lord to speak to me. At the time I was studying a particular devotional titled *Help from the Lord*. It was on an app I was using at the time, so I don't remember all the specifics, but I wrote down something from one of the devotions. It went something like this: "Allow God to take you to new lands, new opportunities, and new relationships, for it is there that you will encounter the guidance of God." It was that phrase "guidance of God" that really stood out[16] *Guidance* has always been a special word to me, for when you look closely at the word, you will see the words, *God you and I dance.*

In my trips to Niger over the years, I had talked about this idea with my teams—allowing God to be the leader and for us to follow His lead, whatever that looks like. So, this phrase in my devotion spoke to my heart immediately, and I knew that it was from the Lord.

At that point I was willing to accept His invitation to travel with this team to a new land, meet new people, and encounter new opportunities with the Lord guiding us! My heart was also so thankful that the Lord provided this opportunity for us right away. We didn't have to wait for somewhere to serve. The Lord is gracious and faithful!

I led a small team to Anchorage and Seward, Alaska, and we had a great mission serving there. We served at a homeless shelter and shared the gospel in a women's prison, where ten ladies accepted Christ. Many others asked for prayer. We hosted a VBS for three days, cleaned a widow's home, hosted a women's gathering, and spent time with our missionary friends. God truly went before us opening doors. He also, in His loving and personal way, allowed us to serve in some of the same areas that my teams had served in Niger (prisons, widows, VBS).

When we returned home, Jason wanted to hear every detail about the mission and asked if I thought I would go back.

"We will see what doors the Lord opens and closes with Niger," I said.

We continued praying and asking the Lord to show us His will. Restrictions remained in place, so I couldn't return to Niger in October 2021. Jason wanted to go to Alaska and see what I had seen, so we planned a trip for October 2021. We would spend time in Anchorage and in the fishing village of Dillingham. As we served in a homeless shelter and some other amazing places, my heart still longed to be in Niger. I was confused and tears flowed, yet Jason was having the time of his life. He had been hunting and fishing there five times, and he has always loved Alaska.

JASON: After the Niger trip for two that Haley and I took, I was already starting to have some hesitancy about my future in Niger. I was sick, deathly sick, and it scared me. Also, I don't think I realized it at the time, but I had become comfortable with the work in Niger. It had become somewhat of a system for me: lead a team in January, raise money back home, lead board meetings, and invest the money in schools. It was hard work, but God had surrounded me with good board members and a hardworking assistant, Cara, which made things easier. I wasn't spending near the amount of time on all things Niger like I had in the past.

When Haley's June 2021 team got canceled, I was not ready for the disappointment that I witnessed in Haley. She was literally heartbroken. I tried my best to be there for her, but nothing seemed to help. So, I went into "Mr. Fix It" mode and called Rodrigo Rivas in Alaska. Little did I know this would be a life-changing and mission-altering phone call… for me.

PAULINA: My parents are a beautiful picture of a spouse reminding another spouse of what the Lord has said and walking together in that and relying on the Rock, which is Christ. That is what roots them deeply in our family and holds our family together. No matter the challenges and the waves that come, they're building our house on the Rock. Nothing will sway that. And I truly believe that is the Lord.

They both have always had a gung-ho attitude, like, we're going to do what the Lord calls us to do. We're going to walk in that.

HALEY: At the end of our time in Alaska we had been privileged to spend time with some native Alaskan people in Dillingham, and God spoke to my heart through those people. Jason and I were intrigued by their personal stories, how God had protected them and drawn them to Himself. I felt a connection to these people and believed that I could return to work with people who had so generously and tenderly hosted us in their homes.

Once we returned home from Alaska, friends and family continued to ask us what was going on with Niger. Would we be able to go back? We explained that we could go back to Niger, but the Lord seemed to be opening a door for us now in Alaska. We continued to seek the Lord and His guidance, and we prayed that if this was His will that He would continue to show us that.

The Lord calls us to be His disciples and invites us to help spread the gospel here on this earth. A verse that Jason and I try to live out is Matthew 28:19: "Therefore go and make disciples of all nations." The Lord also reminds us that it is *He* who does the work in and through us. He just wants us to be willing and available. I have learned in my years of Bible study that God uses ordinary people who simply *trust Him* and *walk by faith*. In Hebrews 11, we are told of the heroes of faith. Each verse begins with "By faith"as it describes the lives of Abel, Enoch, Noah, Abraham, Isaac, Jacob, Joseph, Moses, Rahab, and others.

Jason and I are ordinary people with hearts willing to be obedient to what the Lord calls us to. My prayer is that every person who reads this book sees themselves as valued and loved in the eyes of God. What is He wanting to do through you? *Surrender* your will to His and allow Him to use you in crazy and amazing ways. There is nothing on this earth that satisfies our souls like serving and sowing seeds into the kingdom of God.

I recently learned in a Bible study what a mustard seed truly is. It is a weed that scatters everywhere when the wind blows. Jesus described the kingdom of heaven as mustard seed in Matthew 13. We as believers are called to be the mustard seed in this world—to share who Jesus is and what He has done in our lives.

So how can you be a mustard seed in your areas of influence? Is He calling you to new lands, new people groups, or new opportunities? Just be open and available to Him; it will be worth it in the end!

The Lord has allowed me to witness many miracles while serving Him in Niger. I have seen and helped deliver babies. I have prayed and seen the Lord provide the exact pair of glasses needed to give a person sight. I have witnessed people accept

Christ as their Savior in a place where it is truly a sacrifice to become a Christian. I have seen babies who were dying become healthy within hours. I have needed a translator, and the Lord provided one from the crowds. I have seen lives changed and salvation occur in the lives of team members. I have watched the Lord provide through so many people over the years the exact needs we had. I have seen airlines give nine travelers a group rate that is supposed to apply to groups of ten or more; I've seen thousands of dollars of overage provided, and many other miracles over the years. I have tasted and seen that the Lord is good!

I want that for you, my family, and all people I encounter. Our race with Jesus will look different than we envisioned or imagined at times, but if we allow Him to lead it will be a beautiful dance that brings Him glory.

JASON: God did begin to reveal to me that Alaska was where He was calling us. Several things became clear right away. One was that Haley and I could serve the Lord together in the same country and cause. And two, we would not sit on the sidelines but instead look to serve. The following list of "confirmations" from the Lord were all given to me while Haley was leading the team of four in Alaska for the first time and during the months of July and August after this:

- I was at our hunting property and noticed a metal sign we have had hanging in the bathroom in the cabin. It's been there for probably fifteen years, but

I hadn't noticed it in a long time. It said, "Fly to Alaska."

- When I drove Paulina's car one day, I inadvertently grabbed the keychain that had an Alaska fob on it.
- I was walking into the Publix grocery store behind my restaurant and a little old lady was walking out with an Alaska hat on.
- While in Florida, the following happened to me all within one hour one morning:
    - I got a text about a Chick-fil-A connection who had lost his wife and daughter in a plane crash in Alaska. I immediately prayed for this man.
    - Then we were visiting a friend of my mom's, and the man was showing me his gun room, which was covered with books. The first book I saw was about Alaska.
    - Then I asked this eighty-year-old man his life story. He told me that he lived in Florida but suddenly decided to move to Alaska for four years. I was like okay, God, I hear you!!
- When we took Paulina back to college, we stayed in a different hotel than normal. It was on Alaska Drive in Lakewood, Colorado, and we had no idea. I looked out the window of our hotel room, saw the street sign, and almost passed out.

- I took a picture of a cooler I wanted Haley to get me for Christmas that I saw at Bass Pro Shop. The name brand was Cordova. I got home, and three weeks later I decided to look the brand up online to send to Haley. The company was named after Cordova, Alaska, and one of the founders' names was Jason.
- Then two days later I received an email from Alaska magazine, which I have a subscription for, saying you should visit Cordova, Alaska!

Here's one more important confirmation God gave us. As we wrote earlier in the book, when we traveled to Niger in January 2021, we had an opportunity to share news of a $250,000 grant that Effective Ministries had received for Schools for Niger, Africa. To be more precise, the grant was to complete a model school. This had been my hope for SFNA since my first visit to a Nigerien school. If we could provide a school with tile in the classrooms, a library, a soccer complex, a science lab, and painted walls, and then train teachers to do their best work, that school could serve as a model and become the first of many, because the students at that school would meet higher expectations. They would become models themselves.

Now God had provided the funding through a generous family to complete construction. Not only that, but the family who had so generously donated also agreed to continue giving SFNA an amount similar to what we were raising annually through events.

HALEY: It was as if God was saying to us, "It's time, Jason and Haley. I am bringing in someone else to serve My children in Niamey. I need you somewhere else."

We were able to follow God's call in peace to Alaska.

JASON: I began our book with a discussion of the title, *Sink or Sit*. Here's one more reminder not to sit. So many people say, "I am waiting on God." Well, I believe God is waiting on us. He may be waiting on you!

Read Joshua 3:1–17. Joshua had to step *into* the river for the waters to part. In the water!! Not on the shore, and not one toe! But fully step into the water!

Verse 15 tells us that the river was at flood stage. This takes real faith; it takes faith to follow Jesus. Joshua 3:14 says they "broke camp." Have you broken your camp? Are you ready to step into the water? To do this we must trust God. There is no security in what God calls us to do; there is only security in who God is. Why trust God and step into the water? Because you never know what lies in the balance . . . your *yes* can lead to many *yeses*.

You never know where God will lead, but it will be good.

Since God called us to Alaska, we have since started a new nonprofit, along with a board, called WYGO Ministries. We feel so energized and equipped to lead! One thing is for sure, when left with the choice to *Sink or Sit*, Haley and I will always take the chance to walk on water . . . or, frozen water in this situation!

FINAL WORD

Say *yes* to God. You see, when God asks us to do something, our only response as Christians is to be obedient and say *yes*. We must answer the call from Jesus. I don't mean to say that Jesus will call you on the phone, but as Christians, when we are walking with God, we know and understand when He asks us to do something. My favorite book in the Bible is Nehemiah, and I will share my own personal *yes* with you as well as his.

Nehemiah served as a cupbearer to a king. He knew there was a problem. He knew there was a need, so the first thing he did was pray. The Lord spoke through Nehemiah, prompting him to ask the king for permission to go and rebuild the wall around Jerusalem.

I went to Niger for the first time in 2006 after a friend invited me, I prayed, and I said *yes*. When I was there, the Lord spoke two things to me: "Get more people here to see Niger, so they can love the people and share the good news of Jesus Christ. And help raise money to build Christian schools." I felt this call from the Lord and said *yes*. As of 2020 we had a board of nine members who were dedicated and focused on raising money to build Christian schools.

In 2006, we were working with one school. Today we have now partnered with seventeen different schools impacting more than eight thousand students each year. Like Nehemiah, I recognized I would need to connect the hearts of others to the need before asking them to sacrifice their time and energy. I wanted their hearts to be broken for Niger so they would use their hands to build schools and write checks. None of this could have been done without a calling from God and a *yes* from others.

Let's go back to Nehemiah. He knew he would need others to help. Like Nehemiah, I knew I needed support from others as well. I came back from Niger and invited others to go. After eighteen missions, we have had more than one hundred people associated with Chick-fil-A serve on a mission team in Niger—from operators, to staff members, operator spouses, and team members. Many of these have continued to say *yes* to Niger and *yes* to God over and over.

As Christians we should know that there is something in our hearts or gut that prompts us to move. Christians don't know everything, but we should know enough to act. Even if you lack in experience, you can make up for it with the passion of your heart and the Holy Spirit guiding you.

On my first mission to Niger, I saw a need. I answered God's call. I said *yes*! Since that *yes*, Haley has gone to Niger sixteen times and led numerous women's teams, our three kids have gone three times to serve on mission teams, and we adopted Rachid (and seven more children have now been adopted from that same orphanage). God called us and we said *yes*!

So when God calls you to do something, you must be obedient. The first thing we must do is take time to pray. Each step of the way we must seek the Lord for direction. God will not abandon you. The people of Jerusalem saw this and believed it as Nehemiah rebuilt the wall in record time. So here is my question for each of you today. What is God calling you to do? Have you said yes? We must be obedient because He calls us to be. We must say *yes* because we never know what God's plan is in the yes. One *yes* can lead to so many things. Don't stay on the sidelines or seated in the boat. Wouldn't you rather risk sinking than sitting? Keep saying *yes* to Jesus!

ACKNOWLEDGMENTS

W e want to say thank you to our three children, Rachid, Hunter, and Paulina, for speaking into this project, praying for us, and supporting us as we followed God's call to write *Sink or Sit*.

The Lord has blessed us with encouraging and supportive friends. These friends have been the Aaron and Hur in our life journey of following Jesus and spreading the gospel around the world: "When Moses' hands grew tired, they took a stone and put it under him and he sat on it. Aaron and Hur held his hands up–one on one side, one on the other–so that his hands remained steady till sunset" (Exod. 17:12). These friends are Lawson Bailey, Debbie Bennett, Kristi

Collett, Cheryl Hash, Kelli Nichols, Brad and Derain Roper, and Sharon Thaler.

A special thank-you to our family. Especially our parents for always being so supportive: Jim and Cindy Bilotti and Jackie Martin. Thanks to Cara Brown for going to Niger and Alaska, helping with the kids, and serving at our Chick-fil-A restaurants.

We want to thank our coauthor, Dick Parker, for believing in us and wanting to get our story in writing.

Thank you to Jeff Henderson for being willing to write the foreword and support the book.

May Jesus Christ be glorified with every word that has been written on the pages of this book. Our prayer is that each of you is obedient to God's call. Take a chance to walk on water by choosing sinking over sitting.

ENDNOTES

1 Eddie Van Halen, Alex Van Halen, Michael Anthony, David Lee Roth, "Jump," *Live: Right Here, Right Now*, Warner Brothers, 1993.
2 Otis Redding and Steve Cropper, "(Sitting on) the Dock of the Bay," BMG Rights Management, Universal Music Publishing Group, 1968.
3 Mark Batterson, *In a Pit with a Lion on a Snowy Day* (Colorado Springs: Multnomah, 2016), pg. 114.
4 Batterson, *In a Pit*, pg. 114.
5 John Piper, *Let the Nations Be Glad!: The Supremacy of God in Missions* (Ada, MI: Baker, 2010), pg. 61.
6 Mark Batterson, *In a Pit with a Lion on a Snowy Day* (Colorado Springs: Multnomah, 2016), pg. 128.
7 Margaret Feinberg, *Fight Back with Joy* (Nashville: LifeWay, 2014), pg. 96.
8 Robert Lupton, *Toxic Charity: How Churches and Charities Hurt Those They Help (And How to Reverse It)*, (New York: HarperCollins, 2011), pg. 4–5.
9 Lupton, *Toxic Charity*, page unknown.
10 Brenton Brown and Ken Riley, "Everlasting God," Thank You Music Ltd., 2005.
11 Mark Batterson, *The Circle Maker* (Grand Rapids, MI: Zondervan, 2011), pg. 13.
12 Jason Ingram, Matt Redman, Tim Wanstall, "Never Once," So Essential Tunes, Spirit Nashville Three, 2011.

13 Endurance. Merriam-Webster.
14 Batterson, *In a Pit*, pg. 109.
15 Warren Wiersbe, *On Being a Servant of God* (Grand Rapids: Baker Books, 2007). page unknown.